Buy the Little Ones a Dolly

A MEMOIR

Kate,

May angels always
be with you on
your life's journey.

Rose

7-26-18

Buy the Little Ones a Dolly

A MEMOIR

Rose E. Bingham

HenschelHAUS Publishing
Milwaukee, Wisconsin

Published by
HenschelHAUS Publishing, Inc.
www.henschelhausbooks.com

ISBN: 978159598-566-8
E-ISBN: 978159598-567-5
LCCN: P2017956888

Cover design by Melissa Lee Johnson
Layout by Kevin Gardner

Printed in the United States of America

Dedication

This is dedicated to Grandma Debovik, my mom's mother, who taught me a valuable lesson.

I was under the age of ten. I was wearing bib over-alls, my hair in pigtails, and sitting under an oak tree at the farm, making mud pies. Grandma was sitting in a chair next to me knitting.

I noticed a spider crawling toward me. Grandma must have noticed it as well, because, as I was about to swat the spider, she grasped my raised hand.

"What did that spider do to you?" she asked.

"Nothing."

"That is a daddy-long-legs spider. He eats insects. As you grow up, try and find the good in people and things."

Little did she know how that incident would influence my life, but maybe she did.

The Labyrinth Prayer

Y ou are on the path ... exactly where you are meant to be right now. From here, you can only go forward, shaping your life story into a magnificent tale of triumph, of healing, of courage, of beauty, of wisdom, of power, of dignity, and of love.

—Caroline Adams

Table of Contents

Foreword... 1

Prologue... 3

Chapter 1

A Very Special Thanksgiving....................................... 5

Chapter 2

It Was Not an Ordinary Day... 13

Chapter 3

Teenager to Substitute Mother..................................... 19

Chapter 4

I'd Like You to Meet My Mom and Dad....................... 23

Chapter 5

Life Goes On.. 31

Chapter 6

The Letter With No Return Address............................. 41

Chapter 7

Competition Between School, Friendships,

and Childcare... 45

Chapter 8

The Christmas Letter, and Still No Return Address... 49

Chapter 9

Beginning a New Year... 53

Chapter 10

Junior Prom.. 57

Chapter 11

Frustrations.. 61

Chapter 12

The Summer of 1953–Growing Pains........................... 65

Chapter 13
    Life is Not Static.. 75
Chapter 14
    Blessings in Disguise... 81
Chapter 15
    Transitions.. 91
Chapter 16
    Dreams Do Come True... 97
Chapter 17
    Post High School Graduation.. 99
Chapter 18
    Nursing School, Etcetera... 107
Chapter 19
    A New Life as Mrs. Michael Bingham............................ 131
Chapter 20
    The Sixties.. 139
Chapter 21
    The Seventies, Eighties, and Nineties............................ 153
Chapter 22
    Being a Sister Instead of a Mother.................................. 165
Chapter 23
    The Sisters' Journey as Written in
    My Travel Journal.. 171
Chapter 24
    They Called Her "Mema".. 181
Chapter 25
    Closure.. 187
Chapter 26
    Filling in the Spaces of Mom's Life................................ 193
Epilogue.. 201
Acknowledgements... 205

About the Author.. 207

Foreword

Occasionally you hear about or read a story of families enduring extraordinary odds to stay together while overcoming adversity, and the story sticks to your bones like honey - and you never want to forget it.

This is one of those stories.

Actually, this is more than one of those stories; this is a memoir of astonishing courage and unparalleled determination. Rose's narrative will renew your faith – no matter how long it has been since you lost it.

I first met Rose in 2013 at our annual Writers' Institute writing conference. Rose received the award for First Place within our conference Poetry contest. Rose continued with her writing and enrolled in a Creative Nonfiction class early the next year. As a student, Rose wanted to know everything she could learn about writing a memoir. I must admit that when I learned of how her mother "went to town and never returned" leaving behind seven children with Rose being the oldest at age 15, I was already hooked into learning more about this unexpected and peculiar incident – and the special family that was involved.

Rose spent her life assuring her and her siblings would remain together as a family even when divided between five foster homes. The book you are now holding in your hands is a testament to one woman's determination and dedication to her family.

In the opening chapter is an account of Mary, Fred, Susan, Barbara, Rita, Patricia and Rose getting together for a very special Thanksgiving to celebrate their lives and the finding of answers about their mother. You will join them and you will learn of the triumphant journey Rose sustained in her life, and while writing and completing this memoir.

Be prepared to be mesmerized by this powerful and moving story. As I mentioned earlier, this one will renew your faith, and you will never forget it.

--Laurie Scheer, Faculty Associate, UW-Madison
Continuing Studies, Madison, WI

Prologue

A memoir could have been written by my mother, father, or any of my siblings, Mary Ann, Fred, Susan, Barbara, Rita, or Patricia. Each story would be different. This is my story, with my memories, my assumptions, and my feelings.

Chapter 1
A Very Special Thanksgiving

Life is sometimes threatening like fallen hot wires after a storm,
but beauty can be seen in their sparks dancing on the
wet pavement. –Rose Bingham

Electricity filled the house two to three days before the planned event of a Thanksgiving dinner on Thursday, November 21, 2013, with all seven of us present, something that had not happened since 1951. New dishes and fall-colored tablecloths were purchased, crystal was washed, and entrée assignments given: Patricia would bring the appetizers; Barbara, green bean casserole; Rita, an appropriate wine; Susan, the pies; Fred, squash from his garden; Mary, dinner rolls and cranberry relish; and I would prepare the turkey with the help of Shirley, my brother's special lady.

Rita and husband, Alex, traveled from Orangeville, Ontario and arrived two days before. Alex, an only child, and the father of one daughter from a previous marriage, always was in awe of the size of our family. I think his biggest challenge was coping with the noise level, which is normal at large family gatherings, but rather daunting if you are not accustomed to it.

Fred and Shirley also came a couple days early in order to help me with the preparations. We sibs exchange names at Christmas, and Fred and Shirley had Mike's and my name so they brought an early present, an electric roaster with the capacity for up to a twenty-four pound turkey. I was delighted.

My youngest sister, Patricia, and her husband, Bob, came from Big Lake, Alaska. They visit Wisconsin at least once a year traveling in their motor home or by air. Their visits are usually three-fold: visiting family, checking on property they own, and if in the fall, Bob goes deer hunting.

Bob brought Patricia to the house the day before our family get-together. He visited awhile, then headed north to his cousin's deer camp. We would miss him at our event, but I also understood traditions.

Patricia enjoys entertaining so I appreciated having her as my assistant. I actually had several assistants. Michelle, my oldest daughter, was living with us at the time and had a background in catering and served as a cook in the army. She not only offered to make the turkey stuffing but also helped set up appetizer trays. Between her and Patricia, I suspected the presentation of the appetizers would be like an artist's palette.

*   *   *

"Over the river and through the woods, to Grandmother's house we go." Thursday, November 21, has arrived. It is the week before the official Thanksgiving holiday, but today will be a special thanksgiving for the seven of us. I can feel it. Our log home is on two acres of land, mostly pine and oak woods, and is located eight miles from the city of Wisconsin Dells, and if one travels through the Dells you do cross the Wisconsin River, so I believe the quoted verse is appropriate.

This day is happening because Shirley asked the question, "When did the seven of you, *all* seven of you, last celebrate Thanksgiving *together*?" My reply was, "Probably in 1951, the year before Mom left." Shirley's question is responsible for today's celebration.

Shirley and I arise early to prepare the turkey and get it in the roasting pan. *Mom, I remember you stuffing the turkey with sage dressing. We still have sage dressing, but I make it in a casserole dish, safety precautions, they call it. I especially remember your mincemeat pie. Would you believe it? Mincemeat is bought at the store, and not even near as good as what you and Grandma canned.*

The rest of the houseguests are making themselves present one by one. Fred is in the garage smoking his pipe, a wonderful sweet aroma, but a habit I wish he'd give up. My husband, Mike, is asking what anyone would like for breakfast. One would be foolish not to take him up on his offer. He makes the best eggs and bacon breakfasts ever. Alex appears in his robe, hair still damp from his shower, asking what all the commotion is, as only he can ask. We ask where Rita is. Alex responds, "She is still trying to wake up." Chuckles are heard, and someone says, "Beauty sleep, Alex. It's called beauty sleep."

It isn't too much later, and we hear, "Do I smell bacon?" It's Rita coming from the lower level.

Rylee, my dog, is lying stretched out full length taking everything in with a questionable look in his eyes, I mean *eye*, as he has only one. He lost his eye when a neighbor backed out of our driveway and hit him.

"More coffee, anyone?"

"Good morning!" I hear, as my daughter, Michelle, enters the kitchen.

My husband retorts with his favorite saying, "Don't you know people die in bed?"

"Oh, Dad!"

Patricia appears, looking rested and ready for the day, "Hi, everybody."

Fred walks into the kitchen from the garage and makes a comment about the kitchen and dining area getting a little crowded. I respond, "This is only half of us. Wait until the others show up."

It's late morning and I hear someone at the front door and an excited, "We're here."

It's my sister, Mary, and her husband, Larry, from Green Bay, which is two and a half hours north of us. Her face is full of smiles as she sees her sisters, Patricia and Rita, and her brother, Fred, whom she doesn't see as often. After an exchange of hugs, it's not long before she starts picture taking. As I'm busying myself in the kitchen, I hear a pleading voice, "Come on, Rose." I'm seventy-six, but even at age six, seven, whatever, I was not good with posed pictures, especially on my birthdays. On my sixth birthday, I hid under the bed and was bribed by my Uncle Bud who offered me a nickel to come out. It's weird because I like giving attention to others but I don't like it directed at me, but I do like praise. I'm also a photography guru. Psychologists, figure that one out. Well, let's get back to the party, and by the way, I posed for photos.

My sister, Barbara, and her husband, Woodrow, familiarly known as Woody, arrive from Minocqua, a beautiful community located in Northern Wisconsin. *I am so proud of Barbara. She puts in hours of volunteer time in her community and has the distinction of being a driving force in establishing a homeless shelter in her area.* Barbara has her arms filled with all the fixings for making green bean casserole with onion ring topping. Fred is quick to call out, "Hi, little sister." After setting her things on the kitchen counter, she makes her way toward him for a hug, as well as to Patricia, Rita and Mary. Excitement is mounting. The fragrance of turkey fills the air stimulating salivary juices. An exquisite perfume could not compete.

My sister, Susan, and her husband, John, arrive from Wausau. She is the sunshine of our family, and the pie maker. As she walks into the foyer, I give a sideway hug trying not to dislodge the pumpkin and apple pies she is carrying. John gives me a big hug. John is an only child, so like Alex; he too, is in awe of our family gatherings. Susan, with pies looking too beautiful to eat, still in hand, scans the room to see who else has arrived and exclaims, "This is great!"

I walk over to an area off the kitchen where I have set up a spot for desserts. "Sue, bring the pies over here." She sets them down, and is wearing a smile showing pride in the beauty of her culinary handiwork. She squeezes her arms to her sides, gives a little back and forth wiggle, and I know all is good. "Rose, this is so special," and off she goes hugging each and every family member. More photos, and more photos, and more photos are taken. My cheeks feel molded like a smiling Mona Lisa in a wax museum.

"Excuse me for a moment. I hear someone at the front door." As I approach the door and look through the decorative glass panel, I can make out my niece, Rebecca, who is Mary and Larry's daughter. A few weeks ago she had called and asked if she could join the celebration. She expressed excitement at the chance of seeing all seven of her Steinmetz aunts and uncle together.

"Rebecca, I'm so happy to see you. Last, but not least." She lets out with one of her expressive giggles and exclaims, "Aunt Rose, I'm so happy I can be part of today's festivities."

A traffic cop is needed in the kitchen, but we are managing, finding our own spot to do our part for the meal preparation. Michelle and Patricia are busy setting up hors d'oeuvres including Alaskan salmon.

Deer season is approaching so conversation can be heard among the guys on the topic of hunting. Alex is vegetarian so he reluctantly tolerates the deer talk, making a few remarks as only he can do with his wonderful sense of humor, expressive face, and Scottish accent.

John steps out onto the deck to pop the champagne cork. John is tall and has his long arms stretched out and hands gripping the bottle. He tries popping the cork—nothing happens. He makes another attempt and nothing. All eyes are on him now. Do we need dynamite? And then we hear the familiar pop sound. We are cheering. Glasses are filled. My brother, Fred, is saying, "I'd like to make a toast. Thanks, Sis for having us, and I thank my Shirley for suggesting this get-together. I love you guys." I see him wiping a tear from his face. "And today I'm also thinking of our half-sister, Linda. Wish we would have had the chance to meet her."

As the oldest, I give the second toast: "I too want to thank Shirley. Shirley, you are our other sister and we love you. We've been through a lot but we made it. I thank all the spouses for coming and making this a special day. I believe we can get seated now for dinner."

A table is set up in the living room for Rebecca, Michelle, and the spouses, with the exception of Mike. In the dining room, which is visible from the living room, the seven of us sibs (Mary, Fred, Susan, Barbara, Rita, Patricia, and myself), and my husband, Mike, sit down. We say grace and begin our Thanksgiving feast of roast turkey, dressing, squash from Fred and Shirley's garden, green bean casserole, relishes, cranberries, and hot rolls. It suddenly becomes quieter as all are satisfying their appetites, and savoring this time together.

Mom and Dad, I know you would be proud of us. We are a special bunch and a big bunch. To date, you have twen-ty-three grandchildren, thirty-five great-grandchildren, and nine great-great-grandchildren. Mom, we are family and it's all I ever wished for after you left.

We decide unanimously we will put off having dessert until later.

Patricia announces that I, being the oldest, come and sit in the recliner, and requests the others to gather around. She leaves the room for a moment and comes back with a large flat item in a plastic bag. As I unwrap the package, my guess is, it's a painting since Patricia is an accomplished artist. The bag falls away from the painting, and I am breathless and shaking, and tears are welling up in my eyes. I hear my brother and sisters asking me to turn it around.

"Oh, my, words cannot express what I am feeling." I lower my head and cover my face with the palms of my hands, the painting resting against my legs.

"Rose, let us see."

I turn the painting around, and see the emotions *I am feeling* being multiplied within the room. If those emotions could be weighed, they'd weigh a ton. It's a painting of Mom, with a beautiful smile on her face, graceful fingers extended, reaching for iridescent blown bubbles. Patricia is telling us it took her six months to do an oil painting from a photo and there are copies for each of us. We are hugging and crying and expressing our gratitude. All our beating hearts are one heart.

After drying our eyes, the seven of us pose for several photos in front of the fireplace. Someone is suggesting we pose holding the wishbone. We are all trying to grasp the ends of the wishbone, four on one side, and three on the other. Cameras are focused on us as we make a wish, count to three and pull. To our disbelief the wishbone breaks exactly down the middle. Now we are laughing uncontrollably instead of crying. The two halves of the wishbone will have a prominent spot in my china hutch. We return to the kitchen to clean up. My Mike has a head start on the dishes, but we all pitch in however we can.

We sit down to dessert and Susan's pies are delectable. Conversations center on the wonderful day it has been, the painting, the wishbone, and gratefulness for the way our lives have turned out.

Mom left us, but the threads of our family tapestry were never broken, just frayed at times. Tonight before I fall asleep, I am thinking back sixty-one years ago, when I was terrified as to what would happen to the seven of us.

Chapter 2
It Was Not an Ordinary Day

June 2, 1952,—I was fourteen years old in 1952, almost fifteen. I lived in Camp Douglas, Wisconsin, a community in the lower third of the state. It was the start of summer vacation. Vacation time was fun in a small town because everyone knew one another. It was great going as a group to the swimming hole at Mill Bluff, or watching an outdoor movie on Saturday night, set up on our town street. When not with a group or my family I enjoyed spending time with my best friend, Barbara. We were soul mates. She had the gift of gab and I had the gift of listening so we complemented one another. My little sister thought it was special that she had the same name.

I was sleeping in and awakened by my mother's voice. She sounded like she was at the foot of the stairs. "Rose, I need to go to New Lisbon to the appliance store. I'm going to catch the Greyhound bus and I'll be taking the 3:30 train home. I've made a list of some things you can get ready for Dad's birthday." Sleepily, I answered, "Okay, Mom."

She added, "Take good care of the kiddies."

One of the chores on the list was to iron the starched and dampened dresses for the little ones, Barbara, 5, Rita, 4, and Patricia, 3. Another task was baking my dad's birthday cake. I remember that it was hard to see the frosting when I put on the 43 candles.

I don't recall what my six siblings were doing that day, probably because it was supposed to be just an ordinary day.

Mary, 12, was most likely reading, or roller skating around the corner from our house where the sidewalks began. She loved the skates she had received for her 12th birthday in April. When she skated, her pigtails would be a flying, her skate key swinging on a string around her neck, her body forward with arms outstretched, anticipating each bump between the sections of the sidewalk, as well as any uneven concrete. Freddy, almost 11, and Susan, almost 8, would be exploring at the base of the bluff next to our house; and the three littlest would be playing with their dolls or toys. I know for certain Barbara, or Barbie, as we called her, would have had her doll. She carried it everywhere.

By the time Dad was dropped off from his job at Camp McCoy at 5:30 p.m., I'd already asked myself questions and was worried. *Did Mom miss the train? If so, how would she get home? What about Dad's birthday supper?* Dad walked into the house, set his metal lunch bucket on the table, and knew by looking at us that something was wrong. "Where is your mom?"

Little Rita interrupted his question. "Daddy, Daddy, Rosie made you a birthday cake!"

Dad glanced at the cake, still with the questioning look on his face. He asked me again, "Where is your mom?"

"She was going to the appliance store in New Lisbon. She said she'd be back on the 3:30 train."

"What was she wearing?"

I thought to myself, *That's a strange question*.

"I don't know. I was upstairs in bed, but her big purse is on the dresser."

"Did she say anything else?" His voice had escalated.

By then, I was in tears. "Maybe she missed the train. There has to be a good reason why she isn't home yet."

Dad lit up a cigarette and said, "Rose, come with me."

"Where to?"

"Down to Target Bluff. Mary, keep an eye on the little ones."

We walked to a highway restaurant about a half mile from our home and Dad asked permission to use the phone. We didn't have a telephone or a car. The first person called was his sister, Mabel, who lived in New Lisbon, but since Mabel didn't have a phone, Dad called her neighbor, Mr. Larsen, who was willing to run across the street to tell her she had a call.

"Mabel, this is Fred. Did you see Eleanor today? She told Rosie she was going to the appliance store, but didn't come home on the 3:30 train as planned."

"Mabel, you say, don't worry, but where could she be?"

I could feel people in the restaurant looking over at us, their grim expressions sensing my dad's concern. We were no more than three feet away from the tables. I looked around to see if I knew anyone—they appeared to be all tourists. I pushed myself further into the corner where the phone was located, wishing to be invisible. Dad snuffed out one cigarette and immediately lit another. The combination of the aromas of food and cigarette smoke, no supper, and the worry about Mom, made me feel sick inside.

Dad called the Greyhound Bus Company. He often used the Greyhound for transportation and knew several of the drivers who had the Minneapolis, Minnesota to Chicago, Illinois, route. "Hello, this is Fred Steinmetz calling. I'd appreciate it if you could check with the drivers who had the Highway 12/16 route today, and ask if they recall picking up my wife Eleanor in front of our house in Camp Douglas this morning. If it was Frank or John, they would know. This may be nothing, but I need to know if she boarded, and her destination. You can leave a message at Target

Bluff Restaurant. I'll check in with the restaurant staff tomorrow. Thanks."

The last call was to the sheriff's office. Their suggestion was to wait and see if Mom returned.

We walked back to the house in silence. The silence provided a microphone for the sounds around me. Birds made gentle chirping sounds as they settled for the night. Vibrations traveled across my feet as cars and trucks zoomed down the highway. I was aware of my breathing. I wondered if Dad expected something like that to happen. He approached it all with such urgency. I felt like I had a nightmare and just wanted to wake up.

Questions screamed in my head about an incident that had happened a few weeks before. *Did the quarrel between my parents that woke me have anything to do with Mom not coming home today?* My parents never fought, so was shocked when I came down from my bedroom into the dining area, and saw my mom's face very swollen and reddened, especially her nose. Dad must have hit her. She looked so frightened, and her eyes told me she was sorry I was a witness to whatever it was that had occurred. "Please, Dad. Don't hurt Mom." I knelt down and started to recite the "Lord's Prayer." I didn't know what else to do.

"Go back to bed. This is between your mom and me."

I wondered what had made Dad so angry.

The day following that incident, Mom was quieter than usual. I noticed she had used extra make up to cover her bruised cheek, but it didn't hide the swelling. She answered one question I asked of her, "Has Dad ever hit you before?"

"No."

*　　　*　　　*

Did we eat supper after returning from Target Bluff? What about the birthday cake? Maybe the little ones had cake, being too young to understand.

That night as I lay in the bed I shared with my sister Mary, my early morning thoughts of summer vacation seemed distant. Mary and I cried, consoling one another, trying to hold back the sobs, so as not to awaken the younger ones sleeping in the upstairs room next to us. All five slept in that room. There were three beds: Freddy in one, Susie and Barbie in one, and Rita and Patricia in the other.

Our room was simple. It held a metal bed and a vanity table made of two orange crates set on end and spaced a chair width apart. A board lay across the top. Mom bought me pretty material to cover it. A small mirror hung above. One side of the vanity was mine, the other Mary Ann's. On the right side of the vanity were my comb and brush, Jergen's hand lotion, and most important, Noxzema cleansing face cream. I liked its distinctive smell. Behind the vanity curtain, on the shelf, was my prized possession, a Kodak Brownie camera I won in a Roy Rogers "name my horse" contest. Just two days ago I was taking pictures of Mom and the kids outside under the tree. It wouldn't be soon enough until I got them developed. I never wanted so much for photos to turn out.

Mom, where are you? This has been the worst day of my life. I know in my heart you would not leave without a reason. I tried giving Patricia, Barbie, and Rita butterfly kisses like you do, but it wasn't the same.

Dad and Mom's room, now only half occupied, was directly below ours. I wondered what he was thinking and feeling without his "little gnome," by his side. "Little gnome" was Dad's favorite term of endearment for Mom.

Chapter 3
Teenager to Substitute Mother

The next few weeks were chaotic. Dad continued to check with the sheriff's department, as well as with Mom's sisters in Mauston, Wisconsin, and Chicago, Illinois, to no avail. He did hear from the Greyhound Company reporting Mom hadn't been on that bus. News about Mom leaving traveled fast in our small town. There were questions from friends, neighbors, and relatives—if there were answers, we children were unaware.

My sister, Susan, turned eight one week after Mom left. I have no recall after so many years but I hope we made her day special.

Aunt Mabel, a favorite aunt, who was a teacher and on summer break, paid us visits and made sure we had enough to eat in the house.

Another of Dad's sisters, Myrtle, and her husband Emil and son Dick, came from Tomah to see us. Our Aunt Myrtle reminded me of the wicked witch in *The Wizard of Oz*, not that she was wicked, but similar in stature and outwardly nosy. When I'd see her, I'd be reminded of my grandma's advice about finding something good about everyone and everything. The good about Aunt Myrtle was that she cared enough to check in on us. If she asked too many questions I'd just say, "Ask Dad." I did have to instruct my siblings not to ask her about the many hairs on her chin. Uncle Emil never said much, and I felt uncomfortable around him. He would stand too close, sometimes reaching his arm around my shoulder. It probably wasn't anything, but I didn't like it.

Beside the fact that I wondered every waking moment when Mom would be back, I was deeply concerned what was going to happen if she didn't. Dad still had to work, meals had to be made, the little ones needed so much care, and laundry needed to be done. Being the oldest, I had helped Mom with some of those chores but…

Washing clothes was something else. With eight of us, the volume was overwhelming. I don't know how Mom did it. I found out as a teenager there are so many things one takes for granted. I knew how to sort items into whites, light colored, and dark colored; it was the wringer on the Maytag washer that intimidated me. I remembered the time Mom was guiding a piece of clothing into the wringer, and her hand and lower arm went with it. She was screaming, "Hit the release bar!" Recalling the incident made me more careful. Mom always washed Dad's paint overalls last as they were permeated with paint and turpentine. The odor would fill the room. I did like looking at the paint spots on his coveralls, wondering which color covered what wall or sign.

*   *   *

It was fortunate for me that my dad was a saver. When I decided to write my story, I went to the storage area in my home and began going through boxes of my dad's that we had since he passed away in 1978. I knew he kept letters and would write on the envelope the date he received and answered them. Of note, he always neatly opened the letters on the right side with a letter opener. There were a total of 148 letters I had written to him between 1954 and 1978, as well as correspondence from relatives, my siblings (I returned their letters to each of them), and official correspondence.

There was a letter dated June 19, 1952. That was seventeen days after Mom left. The letter was in response to one I must have written asking if this woman, Rosetta, knew anything. I don't remember Rosetta but she must have been an acquaintance of Mom's. The letter was post marked New Richmond, Wisconsin. She was surprised that Mom had left. Rosetta said Mom visited her in April and had planned to stay a week, but after one day, Rosetta suggested she return home. When I think back to that time I believe she was gone for a week. I wonder where she was the rest of the week and if she was contemplating leaving us at that time.

I also came across a letter dated July 29,1952 from an aunt and uncle of mine who lived in Boaz, Wisconsin. Aunt Judy and Uncle Frank ran a sawmill company and were childless. They replied, because of the time they needed to spend at the sawmill, and their age, they wouldn't be able to help take care of any of the little ones.

I must have been desperate in those early weeks wondering what was going to happen when school resumed in September. Who would care for Barbara, Rita, and Patricia, who were not of school age? I felt wedged between the teenage world and the adult world, innocence and complexity.

Dad did hire a housekeeper, but she wasn't with us long. It was more responsibility than she wanted.

One morning, a couple of months after Mom left, I was sitting at our kitchen table drinking a glass of Ovaltine. *I closed my eyes and allowed myself to visualize Mom, the way she would purse her lips to blow a wisp of hair making its way over her eye. I saw her standing over the cook stove savoring the experience of whatever it was she was making, especially her chicken and dumplings, stirring, tasting, seasoning, and tasting again, all the while the house being filled with mouth-watering aromas. She loved to cook.*

I saw her icing a cake. She was rolling wax paper into a cone shape, and filling it with frosting mixed with food coloring for the appropriate tint, creating flowers, leaves, and pretty swirls. Then I saw us kids gathered around the table, each with our pointer finger getting a bit of frosting she purposely left in the mixing bowl, closing our eyes, and slowly licking it off.

I saw her bringing in a basket of clothes from off the clothesline. Nothing quite matched the fragrance of line-dried laundry. She filled a Coke bottle with water, inserted a sprinkler top, and item by item, sprinkled, folded, and rolled each piece to ready for ironing. Many items were cotton and had been starched, and because there were no steam irons, the dampened clothes would be ironed later in the day or the next day. She had the radio on. Johnny Ray was singing, "Cry."

A rap on the door broke my concentration. "Hi, kiddo! How are you doing?"

It was my friend, Barb, *and* my brother and sisters right behind her. They liked her. Barb noticed I'd been crying and placed her hand on my shoulder.

I looked up at her. "Barb, I miss her so much. She's not only my mother, but my best friend."

"I know. I know."

Susie was telling me not to cry. Susie, Susie, a little diamond in the rough; she was such a tomboy, and at the same time, a butterfly flitting in the wind. I reached down and gave her a hug. I turned to Barb. "Friends of Mom's have commented that I have a special connection with children."

"You do, Rose, you do."

"But will it be enough?"

Chapter 4
I'd Like You to Meet My
Mom and Dad

Before I continue with my story, it is important to me for you to know my parents.

Mom, Eleanor Olga Debovik, was born in Illinois, November 14, 1915, to parents of Polish heritage. The family moved to a farm in Mauston, Wisconsin when she was young. She had three stepsisters, two stepbrothers, and a sister. Her mother's first husband, John Czajka, died and she married Damion Debovik.

Mom was a free spirit and shared with me the frustration she felt with the sexist attitudes of the times when she was growing up. She said she often wished she was a boy and/or man so she could do things they did such as playing baseball, and being involved in adventurous activities girls were not supposed to do. She would've liked to have been a nurse but it was discouraged because it was an "unladylike profession."

Mom loved life, nature, animals, the seasons, and holidays which she made special. On Valentine's Day, she showed us children how to make beautiful valentines using paper lace doilies and cutout pictures of flowers and hearts.

We observed the Lenten season per the Catholic rules, which meant no meat on Fridays, no candy or gum, and attendance at Lenten services. When Holy Saturday came (the day before Easter), Mom would bake the traditional hot cross buns, which were such a treat. On Easter Sunday she had us decked out in our new clothes, Easter bonnets and white gloves for the girls. Of course, there was the fun of finding our Easter baskets. Our traditional Easter meal was Virginia ham studded with cloves and adorned with pineapple slices and maraschino cherries. The dessert was a cake in the shape of a lamb.

May Day was great fun. The day before we'd make a little basket constructed of folded paper and put treats in it. We'd go to a favorite neighbor's home, hang the basket on the doorknob, ring the doorbell, and get out of sight. It was fun watching the recipients face light up.

During the month of May we paid tribute to the Blessed Virgin Mary by placing flowers by a statue of her. The flowers were usually tulips, lily of the valley, and dandelions.

When I was growing up parades were popular on Memorial Day and the 4th of July. In a small town it was a chance to see all your neighbors.

Christmas time usually meant a visit to see Santa Claus. Santa was either in a little "Santa house" set up in front of the Mauston courthouse, or in a room in the courthouse. You told him what you wanted for Christmas and also received a bag of treats.

We always hung stockings. We didn't have fancy ones like they have today. In my day you hung one of your long, brown school stockings. You'd receive an apple, an orange, peanuts in the shell, ribbon candy, anise, and a small candy that had a flower design in the middle of it. Santa would come in the evening after we went to bed, which was earlier than usual. We'd wake up, open presents, and go to midnight Mass. Presents usually meant one toy, some clothing, and since Kleenex was not around, you were sure to get some new hankies. If you didn't get hankies from Mom or

Dad, you were sure to get them from Aunt Mabel. My three favorite presents growing up were a Horsman doll I named Susie, a play doctor's kit, and a yellow cardigan sweater.

Some favorite childhood memories: I remember being in the basement of a house I lived in when I was small. Mom was doing laundry and Dad was there as well. Mom was showing me how to blow a bubble with bubble gum. I laughed when she blew a bubble so large it broke and covered her face.

I remember going sledding in our sloped front yard. Mom would lie on the sled and I would lie on top of her hanging on oh so tight. Most likely it was a tiny slope, but to a young child, it was wonderful.

I remember playing the card games, War and Old Maid, and, when older, Monopoly, with Mom and Dad.

I remember Mom teaching me the alphabet before I started first grade. I would get through the letter P but could not think of Q. She told me to think of the word "cutie" to help me remember Q. When I started school and had to recite the alphabet I said...m,n,o,p,cutie,r,...much to the surprise of Sister Mary Ambrose, my teacher.

Mom's favorite songs were: *Sentimental Journey; My Blue Heaven; Don't Fence Me In; and Danny Boy*. She often sang *Danny Boy* when milking cows at her mom and dad's farm.

I have *no* memory of Mom ever raising her voice.

*   *   *

Dad (Frederick Henry Steinmetz) was born June 2, 1909, to parents of Swiss/German descent, being the tenth of eleven children. Three children died in infancy. His mother, Matilda, died when he was four years old. His sister, Mabel, who was in eighth grade at the time, took a leave from school for two years until the youngest started school. She then returned and completed her schooling with honors. She went on to be a schoolteacher.

His father, August, worked for the railroad. He died in 1949 at the age of 78.

The Steinmetz family was well respected in the community of New Lisbon, as noted in my great-grandpa Rudolph Nathan's and grandpa August Steinmetz's obituaries.

There was strict upbringing in the Steinmetz home. Hard work, good grades, and obedience were expected. One of the German standards was, "A place for everything and everything in its place." I heard the phrase many times growing up and I continue to try, but I am a victim of "organized clutter."

Dad received exceptional grades and was artistic. After graduating from high school he attended Normal School, the term used for schools that trained primary school teachers. He didn't pursue a career in teaching, however, but chose to do high-risk painting, as well as sign painting for business establishments, and lettering on commercial vehicles. He took much pride in his work. You could call him a perfectionist.

The teacher in my dad never left. I learned not to say I was bored. He'd have me get the dictionary, open it, and without looking, place my pointer finger on a word. I was instructed to write the word and its definition three times, read what I wrote out loud, and then construct a sentence using the word. I'm sure that exercise contributed to my being in spelling bees.

He loved crossword puzzles, the more challenging the better. Being an avid reader, Dad was well versed on many subjects. He enjoyed reading to us when we were little. I especially remember him reading *Pinocchio*. If he was going out on the road, we might have to wait two weeks for the next chapter, and I believe that was his connection to us while he was away.

His gardening was a work of art, the rows straight and evenly spaced. A weed wouldn't have dared enter his garden. Sufficient mulch and watchful eyes prevented weeds from happening.

Record-keeping was second nature to him. Much information was noted on a calendar, such as temperature and weather conditions, arrival of birds, chores completed, birthdays, anniversaries, deaths, and appointments, and at the end of a year, it would read like a journal.

Sometimes on the 4th of July, Dad would provide our own fireworks show with fireworks purchased on his painting road trips in other states. As children we eagerly awaited darkness. We'd be seated on the lawn, behind an imaginary line, the "safety line," and Dad distanced himself to the set-up area. Through the evening shadows you'd see him carefully arranging the various types of fireworks. Neighborhood children would call out, "Mr. Steinmetz, can we please come over and watch?"

"Only if you sit in the safe area."

The magic moment would come, almost holding our breath in anticipation, then the oohs and ahs, and holding our hands over our ears but yet wanting to hear, and then, the sulphur smell; you knew fireworks were finished until the next year.

*   *   *

Dad met Mom when he came to work as a farm hand for her parents. They were married August 29, 1936, at

St. Patrick's Church in Mauston, Wisconsin, and were the parents of seven children, all born in Mauston:

Rose Eleanor—July 19, 1937
Mary Ann—April 19, 1940
Frederick Lawrence—July 14, 1941
Susan Audrey—June 9, 1944
Barbara Colette—February 7, 1947
Rita Ann—May 6, 1948
Patricia Lynn—May 10, 1949

*   *   *

Dad's painting profession required travel to other states, such as Illinois, Indiana, and Texas. In 1949, Dad fell in love with the Southwest while doing a job assignment in Waco, Texas. He found a home in Texarkana, a border town of Texas and Arkansas, and signed an Intent To Purchase agreement.

On his return home, the Greyhound bus was involved in an accident. Dad hit his head on a metal bar behind the bus driver's seat. Several months later, in March of 1950, he began having severe headaches and sought medical attention at the local hospital in the city of Mauston where we resided. The physician made the decision to transfer him to Wisconsin General Hospital in Madison, Wisconsin. A brain tumor was ruled out but the headaches persisted. At the end of April 1950, he underwent brain surgery and was found to have two blood clots as a result of the head injury. His speech and motor function was impaired temporarily but returned 100 percent.

The move to Arkansas was canceled. While Dad was unemployed, Mom worked part-time as a waitress and cook at a truck stop.

In August 1950 we moved to Camp Douglas, sixteen miles west of Mauston, so Dad could be closer to Camp McCoy (an army base) where he was to be employed as a painter.

I was 13, Mary 10, Fred 9, Susan 6, Barbara 3, Rita 2, and Patricia 1.

It was hard leaving Mauston and our friends. I had attended St. Patrick's Catholic School and would miss the nuns, and wondered how I'd be accepted in the public school. The public school kids in Mauston often called us "catlickers" (Catholics). The good news about the move was that my friend Barbara and her family, who had lived in Mauston, and then moved to Arizona because of her mom's asthma, had moved back to Wisconsin—Camp Douglas, Wisconsin.

Highway 12/16 passed in front of the house my parents rented. The house was situated next to a bluff that became our playground. When we stepped out of our two-story house, the pine trees covering the bluff filled the air with fragrance. Giant-sized wild blueberries were abundant. Airplanes going over Camp Williams Air Base, which was just across the highway, often interrupted the tranquility of the bluff.

Camp Douglas was now our home.

Chapter 5
Life Goes On

The end of July came and the blueberries were ripe and plentiful. I made sure the kids had on long pants and long-sleeved shirts if by chance there were mosquitoes, and off we went carrying our pails. Blueberries grow at the edge of the woods where they get sun but not too much. Blueberries were easy to pick, and if you placed the pail directly under the clump of berries and grasped them with your fingers, you'd get a handful all at once. I'd remind the little ones, "No green ones, just blue." It was evident they were eating as well as picking; the blue lips gave them away.

After returning home we placed some of the fruit into berry baskets and sold them. Highway 12/16 went past our house, and tourists were delighted to stop and purchase *fresh Wisconsin blueberries* for a quarter a box. We were happy because we had spending money. The remainder of the berries was canned. I followed Mom's recipe book and learned to first sterilize the jars, pack the fruit, and process the jars in a water bath. I was so relieved when the *jars sealed with a pop*.

I had to wait for weekends to do things with my teenage friends, but it wasn't a given just because Dad was home. Barbara would come over and ask if I could get away. Dad often was outside doing yard work, or at the entrance of the cellar, which was on the side of the house, cleaning paintbrushes, or repairing something or other, totally absorbed in his work. I'd be hesitant to interrupt him, so I'd stand there, and all the while praying that he would notice me.

On one occasion, without raising his head, he said, "Yes?"

"Can I go to Barb's house for a couple of hours? Barbie, Rita, and Patricia are taking their afternoon nap, and Mary, Fred, and Susan are playing out front." It seemed forever until he said yes. There were instances when he said no without any explanation. "No" was "no" and that was that.

One day as Barb and I walked to her side of town, the conversation was first about how our family was doing, followed by the latest goings on in town. She was excited to tell me about her neighbor's grandson who was visiting for two weeks. "Rose, his name is Richard and he's *sooo* handsome. He goes by 'Red.' And can you believe it? He attends a military school. The guys in town are going to have their noses out of joint."

I looked up at Barb. She was two years younger, but at least three inches taller. "I can hardly wait to meet him."

"Maybe you'll get a chance today."

As we walked down the street we passed our school principal's house. Mr. Bushman was leaving this area, and Miss Barron, the current English teacher and librarian, was taking over in September. My sister, Mary, became close friends with his daughter, Bobbie, and I used to earn 25 cents mowing his yard. I wondered if the new homeowners would need someone.

We crossed the railway tracks and stopped briefly in the railway station in hopes the stationmaster was sending a telegraph. We were fascinated by the sound—dit, dit, dit, dot, dot, dit. We couldn't exit the station without buying Beemans gum out of the machine.

We passed Kannenberg's Bar. Mrs. Kannenberg often let her son, Duane, invite several of us to their place to watch television. Not many residents had television so it was a treat. Back then programs were broadcast only at certain times of the day.

"Barb, I need to stop at Singleton's store and drop off a film cartridge. I've wanted to do this for weeks. It has pictures on it of Mom and Dad and my brother and sisters that I took the weekend before she left."

"Was that the day I was there?"

"Yes, there should be a couple of photos of you with the kids."

After we dropped off the film, we walked down the tree-lined street toward Barb's house. Sounds of children playing and rotary lawn mowers could be heard. The air was filled with the smell of fresh mown grass; I breathed in deeply, in awe of nature's perfume.

The moment we entered Barb's house, I knew her mom had done her Saturday baking. The house was filled with the aroma of bread, and molasses cookies.

Edie, Barb's mom, stopped what she was doing and gave me an extra-long hug.

"Thanks, Mrs. Brown, for the baked goods you sent over last week. They were gone in no time. I've been making a few things, but I'll never be the cook Mom was."

"Just keep at it, you'll surprise yourself."

I noticed Barb's older sister Patricia was sewing. She was so creative. Her other sister Mary was doing her nails, and Mike, her little brother, was just being a boy. Mike was the same age as my sister Susie.

We sat at the kitchen table and enjoyed milk and molasses cookies.

"Do you want to go over to Green's and meet Dreamboy?" Barb asked, followed by her hearty laugh.

"Okay."

"Rose, before you go home, come back and get a loaf of bread for your family."

"I will and thanks so much."

We walked over to the Green's. Barb knocked on the door and when Mrs. Green appeared asked if Richard was there.

"Yes, he is. Come on in, girls."

And there he was standing behind his aunt. I noticed his eyes immediately, so warm and caring, and he stood so erect. That must be a result of military school.

"Richard, I'd like you to meet my best friend, Rose."

"Hi, Rose, Barb has told me about you."

I said hello and wondered to myself how much Barb had told him about me. Knowing my friend, she'd wait and let me tell what I wanted to tell.

"Call me Red. 'Richard' is just used at school." Barb had told me that, but saying, 'Red' was like I knew him all my life, and not just meeting him for the first time.

"Where're you from and what year of school are you in?" I asked.

"Waukegan, Illinois, and I'll be starting my junior year."

"I'll be a sophomore."

Mrs. Green put her hand on her grandson's shoulder. "It's such a beautiful day. Why don't the three of you go in the backyard and I'll bring you some lemonade?"

As we chatted, it was evident Red was enjoying the quietness of a small town. It didn't take long to know he was intelligent and loved learning, even in the atmosphere of a military boy's school. I shared with him my goal of wanting to be a nurse or a teacher, most likely a nurse. *Am I kidding myself? My goal right now is to make a life without a mother. It was hard holding back the tears. I ached inside. I missed Mom so much and was still a long way from accepting life without a mother.*

I was jolted back to reality, realizing time was ticking away.

"Barb, I'd better head back home."

Red looked at me and said, "My grandmother said I can have some friends over some evening before I return to Waukegan. I hope you'll be able to come."

"Let Barb know."

My mom's disappearance never came up, but I thought Red was someone I could talk to about her. I hoped I would see him again. I liked him.

As promised, Richard, I meant Red, had several of us at his house (*I was overjoyed that Dad said yes*) for hotdogs, his aunt's homemade potato salad, watermelon, and lemonade from fresh-squeezed lemons. *No frozen concentrate back then.*

Barb was there, as well as our friends, Sally, Bob, Marcia, and another Barb. It wasn't long before they asked how I was doing.

"It's been two months now. My dad keeps checking with the sheriff's department."

Red looked up in surprise. Barb must not have said anything, *nor* his grandparents but maybe they didn't know either. I thought *everyone* knew. I imagined folks meeting each other on the street and saying, "Did you hear about the Steinmetz family? Their mother just up and left. What will happen to those kids?" I wondered too.

When it was time to leave, Red offered to walk me home. I noticed an envious look on some of the girls' faces. I'm sure the look on my face was one of surprise. I'd never had a guy escort me home before. I wasn't what you call beautiful, and I was on the shy side. Maybe it was quiet beauty that he noticed. Whatever the reason, I was pleased, but at the same time wondered what I would say during the 20-minute walk home. The time went quickly. Red seemed genuinely interested in my situation and asked if we could exchange addresses. Neither of us had a piece of paper, so we left it, that the next time I was at Barbara's, I would run over to his grandparents' and get his address, and leave my address as well.

We reached the house. I was okay while we walked, but felt awkward when we stopped. We stood by the wooden fence bordering one side of the property. It wasn't quite dark yet, but cars on the highway already had their lights on, spotlighting us as they traveled west. As I was thanking him, he faced me, gently placed his hands on my shoulders, and surprised me with a gentle kiss, my first.

I walked into the house, not wanting to cleanse my face with Noxzema.

Dad was in the living room listening to the radio. "Thanks, Dad."

Mom, I wish you were home. I want to tell you about my first kiss. It's not the same as kissing you or Dad goodnight. The kiss made me feel warm and tingly.

*　　　*　　　*

In August, the one-week summer catechism classes were held at Saint James Catholic Church. It was fortunate that school age and non-school age kids could attend. Several ladies of the church watched over the little ones, engaging them in activities such as coloring, games, singing, and simple bible stories, while the school-age sessions were in progress. It was a bit of a hike to the church for my three little sisters, but they seemed to enjoy the change of pace and the motherly attention.

In the midst of Dad's worrying about Mom, humor did manage to creep into our lives. A nosy neighbor, who lived on the other side of the fence, often was seen peeping through a knot hole to see what those *Steinmetz kids were doing.* Dad had let her know he didn't appreciate it. One afternoon, Dad was watering plants with a garden hose and sensed that she was doing her thing, and without any hesitation put the hose end in the knothole. There was shrieking and threats coming from her side of the fence, but chuckles of satisfaction from our side. That day we *did not love our neighbors as ourselves.*

Just a week or so before school was to start, Dad announced we had to move. I don't know why, maybe the house had been sold, or the rent increased, or maybe it was just too hard for Dad to stay in a house filled with memories of Mom. All I could think of, was how would Mom find us if she returned.

Packing up for the move kept us busy, so I was thankful the catalog order to Alden's had already been mailed, in preparation for school. Dad had told us to pick out two outfits from the catalog, as well as a pair of shoes. To assure you were getting the right size required standing on a sheet of paper and having someone draw around each foot. The drawing was sent along with the order. It was hardest drawing around Patricia's, Rita's, and Barbara's feet because it would tickle them and then they'd move, and the process would have to be repeated.

We moved across town into a much smaller house. The house must have had walls of elastic to accommodate the eight of us, *as well as* Pepper, our dog, and Inky, our cat. The house had a kitchen, living room, two bedrooms, and a back room used mostly for storage. In one bedroom were placed two beds, foot to foot, with a curtain divider. Barbara, Rita, and Patricia slept in one, and Susan, Mary, and I in the other. These were double beds, not queen; therefore, pillows were placed at the foot and the head. Two of us slept on one end, one on the other. We mastered the positioning of our legs and feet in order to have room, but not without: *your toenails are poking me, or you have all the room, or you have too much blanket.* I think I could write a book on togetherness or the act of bonding.

My brother slept in the other bedroom with my dad. Where else?

It was no wonder that housekeepers didn't last (there were a total of four in two years). The only place left to sleep was on the couch. Helen and Dorothy must have stayed the longest. They are the only two I remember, especially Helen—she chewed tobacco.

Our clothing was kept in the back room. The one closet was in Dad's room.

There was no indoor bathroom, just an outhouse, kindly referred to as the Royal Throne. A morning ritual was emptying the chamber pot which was used during the night, and not the most pleasant job.

Keeping clean was a challenge. A washtub was brought into the kitchen, filled with warm water from the wood stove reservoir, and used as a bathtub. We had to do this in our other house but there was more space to do it. We older children, for privacy's sake, washed ourselves in the back room. There was a sink with a hand pump in the kitchen where we shampooed our hair. I remember putting vinegar in the rinse water so our hair would be *squeaky-clean*. Teeth were brushed with baking soda.

During the school year it was (I may as well say it) a madhouse for all of us to get cleaned, dressed, and fed on time.

Railroad tracks were practically in our backyard. In the beginning it was a full-time job making sure Barbara, Rita, and Patricia stayed a safe distance from the tracks. It was an even bigger job watching Freddie, who thought it'd be a great adventure to hop on and take a ride. Vibrations from the passing freight trains could be felt throughout the house, more noticeable at night when all was quiet. We had our very own orchestra, complete with train whistles, noises from the coupling and uncoupling of cars, and the rhythm only trains can make as they pass through.

Back then I was leery of the *gandy dancers*, seen from our house. Today I know that *gandy dancer* was a slang term used for early railroad workers who laid and maintained the tracks in the years before the work was done by machine.

I paid attention to the train schedule when I planned to hang laundry on the clothesline. If billowy black smoke was present when the train passed the house, the clothes became flecked with little black dots.

Another memory was walking through the sandy yard and being attacked by sand burrs. Heaven forbid, if the shoes you were wearing had shoelaces. Those sand burrs attached themselves to every part of the laces including the loops of the bow. You almost needed a blood transfusion after picking them off with your fingers. Thank goodness for penny loafers. In the spring Dad made sure one section of the property would not sprout sand burrs; he planted a garden.

Somehow we made it through the summer. I was disappointed I was unable to go to Chicago and stay with my cousin, Delores, for a week, as planned before Mom left. Delores and her parents visited me for a day, so all was not lost.

Grandpa Debovik, my mom's dad, visited when Mom's sister, Isabel, and her husband could drive him from Mauston. Grandpa was such a gentle man, the grandfather everyone wished was his or hers. His eyes drew you in, as well as his smile beneath the mustache. When doing farmwork he wore bib overalls and long-sleeved shirts, but when he came to town, he was in dress pants, a suit coat, and a proper hat. His not knowing where his Eleanor was saddened him greatly. He would say, "Ay, ay, ay, what was she thinking?"

Red wrote to me as promised and I answered. Today if I went looking through photos and memorabilia, I am quite sure I would come across a dashing photo of him in his military uniform.

I anticipated the start of my sophomore year and, at the same time, was filled with concern in regard to childcare for my three little sisters. Perfect attendance and good grades were important to me and needed if I was going to be a teacher or nurse. What if Dad was working? What if a housekeeper was not there? What if? What if? What if?

Chapter 6
The Letter with No Return Address

During the first week of September on my way home from school, I made my routine stop at the post office to check for mail. Our postal box was 292. The postmaster who was short, round, and jolly, was a bit like Santa Claus, and usually poked his head through the bank teller-like opening, and greeted me, unless he was sorting mail or waiting on a customer. Even then he would announce, "Just yell out if you need something." In a small town, running a post office was a one-man operation.

The rows of postal boxes were aligned on the far wall, each about 3x5 inches in size with a small window—perfect for taking a sneak peek while pointing the arrow on the dial to the correct numbers. My sneak peek was more than casual as I immediately recognized the handwriting on the envelope. It was Mom's. *Oh, my gosh ... she's coming home ... she's OK.* I recall my hands shaking, interfering with the simple task of opening the door. I pulled out the letter; actually there were two letters, one from Red, which at that point became incidental. Before coming to the post office I had instructed Mary, Fred, and Susan to head on home. I wished they were here and wanted to shout, "We have a letter from Mom!" and hoped they were in earshot.

The envelope was postmarked Englewood, Illinois. No address was written in the left-hand corner. That surprised me. Mom was fussy about having the address, return address, and the stamp all in their correct placement. *Maybe the address is in the inside.*

The letter as written:

I love you kiddies and miss you so—only God knows how much. I've lost 30 lbs. You wouldn't know me. I look so thin.

Chicago, IL
September 1, 1952

Dearest kiddies,

It seems like a million years since that day mummy felt she had to leave. Sure hope this finds you all feeling good and not too unhappy with me gone, was coming home after 3 wks. Then heard that if I came home I was going to be arrested 2 years in jail for each of you kiddies so Mama thought I'd stay away and at least could send you money for little things you like and also for the other kiddies though at times it seems my heart will just break, if I don't come home.

Rosie, I sure hope Daddy wouldn't have been so mean when he was drinking then we would never be parted like this now. I sure hope that someday we'll be together again. Mama is working; I make on the average of $52.00 a week. I stay right here at the restaurant and get my room for $6.00 a week. This is the first chance I had to send any money because as you know I didn't take any clothes so have had to get uniforms and a couple of dresses. Also got me a coat. Sure wish I could give you my address so you could write and tell me how you all are, but if I did that, they'd find me and I'd have to go to jail—so honey we'll just have to let things as they are. Mama will keep on writing and sending you money that's all I can do now to show you kiddies I still love you with all my heart and miss you till it hurts so sometime I don't think I can stand it. But guess that's mummy's punishment for leaving. But honey please think of mama sometime because if I thought you kiddies hated me for leaving I couldn't go on. Before you get this letter I imagine you'll be going to school. I hope you each got new clothes to start school in. Sure hope you have all been well, Mama worries about every one of you. Well darling, be a good girl and Mary and Freddie and all of you, and let's pray to God that someday Mama can see and love you kiddies oh so much and be with you if only for a little while. I'm sorry I couldn't send any money sooner. But that is why I didn't write until I could. Bye now honey for a little while and I'LL write again. So until then God bless all of you and Please God take good care of them for me. That's all I ask.

All my love, Mummy

Mummy is sending $30.00 this time that will buy each of you something nice and promise to send you more just as soon as I can.

I'm sorry darling about your trip here to Chicago have wondered a lot of times if you made it or not, was even tempted to call Aunt Clara. I found her address in the telephone book but was scared to. Have wondered if Delores came out. Oh, if I just knew you were all OK I'd feel much better. This not knowing is driving me crazy.

Mom, how could you think we would be "feeling good and not too unhappy" that you are gone? I don't understand—I just don't understand. Why couldn't you and Dad work things out? With no return address, I am helpless. The little ones don't cry as much as they did in June, but I cry for all of us, and hope, and wish, and pray. Please, please come home. We need you, I need you.

Chapter 7
Competition Between School, Friendships, and Childcare

L iving in a small town and going to a high school with thirty-eight students had its advantages. There was ample opportunity for being involved. For example, the sophomore class had seven students, and elections were held for five class officer positions. During the three years I attended Camp Douglas High School, I held the office of Class President and Secretary. I participated in Pep Club, Forensics, was on the Annual Staff, and assisted in the cafeteria, library, and principal's office. A place on the homecoming court was special because my classmates chose me.

I welcomed being busy so I didn't have to think of Mom's absence and her letter, which seemed so final. Not true—I thought of her every waking moment. I would wake up in the middle of the night thinking of her. I had shared the letter with Dad, but he really didn't say much. I read the letter over and over and over. I would close my eyes and imagine I could hear her voice, but the message seemed clear—she wasn't coming home.

In October of 1952, the principal announced there would be a hayride. LeRoy, who was my age but a freshman, asked if I'd go with him. I had noticed him in the cafeteria and in homeroom; there was a sullen and mysterious look about him. He had a short, slicked-back, typical 1950's haircut. His eyes were prominent. He always looked like he was thinking and had a chip on his shoulder about something. He often wore a brown leather jacket, a jacket that seemed to be a part of him, with well-worn creases at the elbow. When I think about it now, I would say he looked a lot like the actor, James Dean, who appeared in the movie *East of Eden* and *Giant* in about 1955. This actor with so much promise suffered an untimely death due to a car accident.

The night of the hayride, classmates assembled in front of the school community hall, anxiously awaiting the horse-drawn hay wagons. We talked about the upcoming football game and other school related topics. I was quiet as usual and a bit nervous about my date, who was standing by my side. The two wagons arrived and it was a scramble as we climbed up and claimed a space. LeRoy and I sat rather stiffly next to one another.

As the horses started clip-clopping along the road, there was teenage chatter and laughter. Conversation decreased and I became aware of the evening coolness on my face, the rhythmic sound of the horses' hooves, and the sweet scent of fresh cut hay. I sensed our bodies relaxing and the warmth from sitting next to each other. I liked the feeling but also felt guilty. When I was thirteen or fourteen, Mom and Dad had explained the birds and bees to me, but I wondered to myself, "Is it OK to sit this close?"

The hayride was the start of a boyfriend-girlfriend relationship, but not like going steady. I learned that he was at odds with his father, somewhat like my situation with my father, whom I didn't quite know how to approach. It was always so comfortable talking with Mom. So, LeRoy and I connected, which wasn't always a good thing. An inner struggle developed between wanting to be with him and the responsibilities of caring for my sibs.

When you are so lonesome inside and you have teenage hor-
mones at work you cannot over estimate what it means to be walk-
ing with someone of the opposite sex and having that person do
nothing more than look into your eyes and tenderly run a blade
of grass along your face. I felt like I was floating and felt warmth
from the inside out. I wasn't sure how to handle these feelings.

Some sporting events at school I could attend, others I couldn't. So much depended on Dad being home. Often my friend Barbara would stay back from a game and come over and help me with the little ones. I appreciated her loyalty as a friend.

Childcare for my siblings not of school age was inconsistent. Caregivers included a housekeeper when we had one, Mary, our next-door neighbor, or Dad. If none of them were an option, I would first panic, then take a deep breath and take the three little ones in tow and try to solicit a neighbor who would be willing to watch them for the day.

God bless the elderly couple, living a few blocks from us, who would say yes. When I knocked at the door, Mrs. Olson would know why I was there. Often as she opened the door, whiffs of pipe tobacco and home cooking escaped out into the air. Mr. Olson was usually sitting in his rocking chair. Mrs. Olson would gently Patricia the heads of Barbara, Rita, and Patricia saying, "You poor babies. Come in." I'd cringe a little inside. I didn't want her feeling sorry for us. We were doing the best we could.

And there they stood, Barbara, dark-haired, petite, with fine facial features; Rita, with her expressive eyes that pulled you in; and Patricia, with her round little face, blonde hair, and a smile like no other. "Come back, Rosie."

"I'll be right here after school. I promise. Be good little girls."

I would thank Mrs. Olson and run the rest of the way to school so as not to be late.

Mr. and Mrs. Olson were only two of many angels I would have in my life.

I can only imagine what neighbors were thinking as I was trucking down the street in the early morn before the start of school.

Chapter 8

The Christmas Letter, and Still No Return Address

I t was just a day or so before Christmas. My Aunt Mabel drove up from New Lisbon. When I saw her car pull up in front of the house, I assumed she was checking in on us and bringing some gifts (she always gave us a little something like handkerchiefs and socks) but she didn't come for the reasons I thought. She handed me a letter Mom had mailed Special Delivery personally for me but to her address. *Why to her address? Did Mom think I had not received the first one? Did she think Dad got the mail but didn't tell me?* My heart raced. *Could I even hope for the best Christmas present ever?*

I looked first at the postmark, which was New Lenox, Illinois, and Dec. 21, 1952. I was disappointed there was no return address. I opened the envelope with shaking hands. Inside was a Christmas card, a very homey card picturing a blazing fireplace with a wreath above it, a hooked rug, and a rocking chair. The verse inside read: Although you may be "out of sight," You're never "out of mind," That's why these wishes for you are the "loving-ever" kind. Merry Christmas-Happy New Year!

The letter as written:

> Dearest kiddies,
> It's been so long since I wrote to you. But right after

the last letter you got Mummy got laid off and couldn't
find as good a job as I had so couldn't save any money
to send so didn't write unless I could. Haven't been
feeling so good, guess my nerves are shot worrying
about you kids. Am too scared to come home to see
you. It's been an awful lonely world kiddies. Loving
you and wanting you. Especially now at Christmas
time when we always had such a good time together.
Mummy is sending $50.00 she saved up to make it a
little happier even if Mummy can't be there. Maybe
God will let us be together someday—how I hope
and pray. Babies Mama loves you and it isn't easy for
Mama. Don't let anyone tell you Mama has forgotten
you, cause darling children—nobody but God knows
how terribly I miss you, how alone Mama feels every
moment I live away from you. How are my babies?

Rosie, buy them a real nice dolly. I mean Patsy,
Rita, and Barbie, and you bigger kiddies whatever you
need. Sure wish I could have sent a $100.00. Honey
girl, if Mummy had it she sure would. All I want for
Christmas would be to have all you kiddies to myself if
only for an hour. Just to see you all again and love you.
I don't think I could ever let you go, but when I can't
it breaks my heart to even think what an awful lonely
day it's going to be for me.

Has Daddy been good to you? I hope so. It's all
you have, I'm so sorry you poor innocent little things
have to suffer for something that was no fault of yours.
Oh if God could only help me find a way to make up
for all those unhappy hours Mama has caused you by
leaving. Forgive me kiddies just a little bit—but I was
frightened. Still am. Sure hope you get this. Will send it
to Aunt Mabel's. Then I know you will. Wish Grandpa

and all a Merry Christmas. May it be more merry than mine.

Darling Babies, will be with you at Xmas Mass Christmas morning even tho it will have to only be in my heart. Love you all so much, that's why it hurts so. Bye babies mine. Mummy will send you some more money soon as I get some saved up ok? Be good kiddies and God bless you all and keep you all well. I know God will be with you all, cause you're so good— always were. Rosie, kiss them all for Mama please won't you? Love you. Your mother forever.

I don't remember what I purchased for us older kids but I did buy dollies for the little ones as Mom requested. They loved the dollies but couldn't understand they were from Mom when she wasn't there.

This would be the last letter. I didn't know that at the time so continued to hope for the next letter. Ever so often Dad would ask if I heard from her. I couldn't blame him, after all, both letters had been sent to me.

*   *   *

When I went through personal items in 1952 in preparation for writing my memoir, which included this letter, I became aware through notations on the envelope that Dad had been trying to find her. I must have shared the letter with him. The notations included the date the money order was issued December 19, 1952, the issuing employee's initials (EJ), the money order number 7-53,119,635, and the remitter: Mrs. Eleanore Steinmetz. The information Dad wanted was not there: What address given? He had that written on the envelope with a question mark for the answer.

I discovered Aunt Mabel had also tried to make contact. I found returned letters she had sent addressed to: Restaurant Worker Eleanor Steinmetz, both to New Lenox, and Elgin, Illinois.

Chapter 9
Beginning a New Year

1953 was the beginning of a new year without Mom. It still felt like the world had ended but it hadn't; the stars continued to shine, the moon came out, we woke up each morning, and it was what it was, and we tried to make the best of it.

Camp Douglas was surrounded by bluffs but didn't have "sledding hills." There was a small wooded bluff not far from our house. We often used it as a short cut to school. We made it our sledding spot. I recall those times and feel fortunate that I am here to write about it because we virtually maneuvered "cardboard sleds" through the trees.

I would help the kids get into their snow pants, coats, and black boots that went over shoes and buckled. It was no easy task. Picture this: I would already have my bibbed snow pants on but not my coat. Mary, Fred, and Susan could get ready themselves and, of course, were eager to go.

"You need to wait until we are all ready."

Patricia, Rita, and Barbara all wanted to be first.

"Hold still. No, put your leg in this side. Push; push your foot into the boot. Let's try putting your mittens on again. You have two fingers in the same space."

By the time all were dressed I was so hot I didn't want to put on a coat.

Off we would go, joined by other kids in the neighborhood. Once we arrived at the bluff I would position myself on a piece of a cardboard box with the little ones taking turns being straddled between my legs. I would hold onto the sides of the makeshift sled and use my feet for rudders as I threaded through the trees.

There would be sounds of disappointment when I announced, "Time to go home."

Our wool mittens and hats would be covered with miniature snowballs, which were impossible to shake out. The buckles on the boots would be snow packed and iced shut. When the boots were removed it seemed half the snow hill was inside. A small snow pile in the middle of the kitchen, wet wool smell in the air, reddened smiley faces, and soggy cardboard sleds spoke of therapy of the best kind.

I continued to receive letters from Red. I had told him about LeRoy and wasn't surprised when he wrote back saying he was happy I had someone to run around with—that's just who he was.

"Running around" in those days meant walking to school together or hanging out with others. I went squirrel hunting with him one Saturday. He let me fire the gun but I didn't care for that too much. I guess we were seen together often enough that I was considered LeRoy's girl.

Several months after I met LeRoy, rapping on my window awakened me I had to stretch over my sister, Mary, to investigate. Although the voice on the other side of the window was muffled, I knew it was LeRoy. I couldn't believe my eyes. I opened the window a bit.

"What are you doing here?" I whispered so as not to wake my sibs.

"I need to see you."

"What time is it anyway?"

"About ten."

"Why aren't you home in bed and what's so important that it can't wait until morning?"

"I have hardly seen you except walking to school. You're always so busy with school."

"I like school."

"Come out for a little while."

Against my better judgment I slipped on my shoes and threw some warm clothes on over my pajamas. As I climbed out the window, I heard Mary say," You are going to get in so much trouble."

"Not if no one tells."

LeRoy and I leaned against the house, shivering more than talking. There was still snow on the ground. I don't remember what we talked about, but I found myself secretly asking what it was that attracted me to him. School didn't mean to him what it did to me. He would've rather been hunting squirrels, or riding on his uncle's Harley Davidson motorcycle.

Why did I find it exciting to be sneaking out of the house? "LeRoy, I need to go back into the house. I'm freezing." He kissed me and hoisted me back through the window.

The next morning before leaving for school, I stamped out footprints still visible in the snow.

Chapter 10
Junior Prom

I was excited when one of the local ladies offered to teach dancing at no charge. She thought it important that teens learn some basic dancing such as the waltz, fox-trot, and polka. It was held evenings; Dad was home so I was free to participate.

On one particular class night, an upperclassman by the name of Darwin McCumber ("Doc") became my partner. Our instructor strongly believed in rotating partners. We would be dancing and you would hear, "Change partners. Quickly, quickly." There wasn't time to be shy. While dancing with me, Doc surprised me off my feet. "Rose, I'd like you to be my prom queen." I could hardly speak. "I don't believe I can. I'm only a sophomore."

"It's OK. I've asked permission from the principal."

With a smile on my face I answered yes. At that moment I felt like Cinderella. As we continued to dance I am sure I had a worried look on my face wondering how I would be able to buy a prom dress and shoes, *and* how would I explain this to LeRoy.

I didn't know until later that Doc had inquired of my friend Barbara, "Do you think Rose would go with me if I asked her to the prom?"

As I walked home after my dance class, my thoughts were on how I would approach Dad to tell him about the invite. I had the good sense to know money for groceries and rent had a higher priority rating than a prom dress and shoes. I walked into the house and with my fingers crossed behind my back I just blurted out that I had been asked to the prom and would need a dress. I couldn't believe my ears when I heard Dad say, "That's really nice, Rosie. We'll work it out."

And work it out he did. Dad made arrangements with my friend Barb's great-aunt Irene to take me shopping. We drove to Mauston, and went to a woman's shop called Smarts. I had been pleased because I knew Mrs. Smart and her daughter, who was a classmate of mine when I lived in Mauston. Mrs. Smart asked how I liked living in Camp Douglas. When I told her about Mom's disappearance, she was first shocked and then sympathetic. "If there is anything I can help you with, please let me know." I appreciated her kindness.

Once again I felt like Cinderella, trying on lovely dresses and shoes. The dress I chose was a heavenly blue, strapless, floor-length gown. I had never worn anything strapless but Mrs. Smart assured me the dress would stay in place endowed or not endowed. *I hoped she was right*. My shoes were a style called ballerina slippers.

On the night of April 24, Doc came to the house about 5 p.m. I was excited but nervous. I had only known Doc as an upperclassman and a dance partner. Doc looked handsome in his dress shirt, dress pants, and tie. I noticed he was carrying a corsage—a white gardenia, so delicate and with a sweet scent I would not forget. I asked Dad to do the honors of pinning it on my dress. I could tell by the look on his face that he was happy for me. He kissed me on the cheek and wished me a good time. One of the best parts was hearing my brother and sisters telling me how pretty I looked. I looked pretty. I felt pretty. I was pretty. *Mom, I wish you were here.*

We joined the other prom court couples at a local restaurant, the same restaurant where Dad and I had gone to make phone calls the day Mom left. I put those memories aside and enjoyed the experience. It was the first time I ate out at a place other than the A&W or the ice cream parlor. I ordered shrimp, which I'd never had before. With Doc paying for it I knew I had to eat the meal, like it or not, but I enjoyed it thoroughly.

Our prom song was *Stairway to the Stars*. It was a magical evening with the streamers of crepe paper and hundreds of stars suspended over us as we danced, stars that classmates and I had cut out one by one earlier in the day, and again I wished Mom could have seen me.

After the prom festivities we went to Doc's home. The eight of us talked, listened to music, and enjoyed a middle of the night breakfast made by Doc's mom, who made me feel so comfortable. Mom would have enjoyed feeding a group of teenagers—she loved to cook.

Doc escorted me home at 5 a.m. I walked into the house just as Dad was leaving for work.

"Did you have a good time?" he asked with a twinkle in his eye.

"Yes, I did. Thanks, Dad."

Chapter 11
Frustrations

There were times when Dad's frustrations increased and coping abilities decreased. Often the little ones became the target of his frustrations. One rule at the table was you ate whatever you put on your plate. We older kids could judge the portions but not the little ones. On several occasions Dad would force them to eat, when it was obvious to me, a fifteen-year-old, that it was making them sick. Sometimes Dad would add food to what they already could not eat. My heart would be breaking inside. I felt each gagging episode, but most of all the pain of helplessness. When I married and had children I could suggest they finish their meal but not force them.

My dad did some other things that were hard to understand. We had linoleum flooring in the kitchen. I'm sure it was a night he'd been drinking when he had Freddy get up and help him paint the linoleum barn red. It was the first image when you woke up and the last when you went to bed. My friend Barb put a little humor in it by saying, "Look at it this way, Rose. No one else has a floor like that." She was dead right.

It was times like this when I welcomed an invite from Barb to stay overnight at her home or her Aunt Irene's. Her Aunt Irene and Uncle Ralph lived a couple of miles outside of Camp Douglas. Just walking down their driveway was pleasurable. Their home was set back and flanked by mature evergreens. We usually entered the house by the back door that led into a kitchen that always smelled wonderful. Irene loved to bake. One time when we came, there were blueberry pies cooling, and Irene was in town. Barb and I each ate a pie, much to her Aunt Irene's dismay, as they were for ladies who were coming to her home for a meeting. I have not eaten blueberry pie since.

The home had a beautiful dining room, living room, and sun porch. The living room had a piano. Sometimes when I was at the house, Barb and I did chores or ironing. I never tired of running a carpet sweeper over the beautiful floor coverings, or ironing sheets on a mangle. I welcomed taking a bath in a bathtub and then climbing into bed between sweet-smelling sheets. It was amazing how much more space you had when it was two to a bed instead of three.

It was fun staying overnight at Barb's house as well. Barb's room was on the second floor. We would climb out her window onto the roof of the front porch and try to solve the problems of the world. I would talk about the loss of my mom; she would talk about her mom's alcoholism. One night we each pricked our fingers, put them together, and became blood sisters. We vowed we would have the same wedding day and we did, only in different years.

Dad's drinking seemed to increase. He would buy Mogen David wine to drink at home and go to one of the local bars if he wanted to drink beer. If he was late getting home I would sometimes walk downtown with the kids to see if he was in one of the bars. The front window of his favorite bar was too high for me to look into so I would hold up Rita, Barbie, or Patricia and ask if they could see Daddy. Usually it was a "yes." We would try not to be noticed but one time he saw us and came out and ushered us into the bar. I just wanted to die.

"Hey, everyone, I'd like you to meet my kiddies—the **best** in the world." I could tell he was proud to show us off but I didn't feel comfortable being in the bar. Cigarette smoke hung in the air, and the odor made me wonder how the bar patrons could enjoy what they were drinking.

"Come on, Dad. Let's go home. We shouldn't be in here."

"You're with me. It's OK."

"Please, Dad."

He turned toward the bar, emptied his glass in a gulp, put out his cigarette, and off we went.

My dad did other unexpected things that were positive. It was the Christmas of 1953. I don't remember what presents Mary, Freddy, Susan, or I received, but I'll never forget the pretty skirts Barbie, Rita, and Patricia received. Dad had made them on Mom's sewing machine.

Chapter 12
The Summer of 1953
Growing Pains

Without television, all ages gathered in the early evening to play yard games, games that today's youth and teenagers probably haven't heard of or wouldn't think of playing: tag, Red Rover, Starlight Star Bright, and Simon Says. Going barefoot in the summer was not unusual. One night during one of our games, I was running through an uncut grassy area bordering our yard and cut the side of my foot on a tin can with a rolled-back lid. Hardly missing a beat I ran into the house, washed the bleeding cut, poured iodine on it, put on some adhesive tape, and went back to the game—no stitches or tetanus shot. I ended up with a scar in the shape of a musical note, a quarter note, to remind me of that night. My real battle scar was my inner conflict between being a kid and a young adult.

Freddy was the marble champ of Camp Douglas, expanding his collection of steely, cat eyes, aggie, and clay marbles. He welcomed being challenged to a game of marbles, and the knees of his jeans proved it.

On Saturday nights, movies were shown outdoors in a roped-off area on a side street in downtown Camp Douglas. Families would bring blankets to sit on. A cartoon, which my little sisters loved best, was always shown before the main attraction. Mary Ann usually sat with her best friend Vivian, LeRoy's sister. Freddy would be with his friend,

Louie. Susan sat with Barb, the three little ones, and me because Barb had a brother Mike who was nine years old like she was. These were enjoyable evenings and free popcorn was available.

That summer my friend's Aunt Irene came to the rescue once again. Our dog, Pepper, was hit by a car and suffered a broken leg, and Dad didn't have the money it would cost for a veterinarian. Irene saw to it that Pepper was taken care of. Pepper adapted well to his leg splint and healed nicely.

Train cars fascinated Fred and Susan, especially when the train was stopped behind the house. They would crawl up into a vacant car, something they were not supposed to do, and jump when they heard the engines start up. One day that summer, Fred and his friend, Louie, climbed into the car but was unable to jump as the train picked up speed too quickly. They ended up in Tunnel City, seventeen miles away. Fred knew our Uncle Emil lived in Tomah, which was not far from Tunnel City, and had a phone and a car. Uncle Emil's name was familiar as he worked for the railroad, which was in my brother and his friends favor. He was called and went to Camp Douglas, picked up Dad and Louie's dad, and went to retrieve the boys. It was an adventure the boys wouldn't forget nor repeat. Today my brother tells me he was sure he was never going to see home again.

Memories of that summer included Dad's garden, which flourished and provided us with bright red radishes, green peppers, tomatoes, cucumbers, and green beans, as well as beautiful zinnias that we could cut and put in a vase, the vase being a fruit jar. He worked hard turning a sand burr patch into fertile soil.

I turned sixteen that summer. It was a disappointing birthday because my dad, who never forgot anything, forgot my birthday, or most likely had other things on his mind. At the time I was hurt, but now as an adult I understand that he had a job to go to, seven of us to worry about, as well as dealing with the disappearance of his wife and who knows what else. My birthday was insignificant. I walked to my friend Barb's house feeling sorry for myself and was also remembering that Dad had given Mary Ann a cute little purse for her birthday in April. Maybe that is why today I am the official special occasion card giver.

My body had changed physically and emotionally. I had ambivalent feelings about taking care of my sibs. I knew they needed me but I needed to be a teenager. It was a struggle. When I did leave the house I felt like I was sneaking off. Mary Ann and I had the biggest share of the responsibility of watching the others and doing household chores, so conflict arouse when she wanted to go to her best friend Vivian's house and I wanted to be with Barbara, or a group of friends.

I would go to Tomah when I had the chance. It was a bigger community with actual stores you could walk through and dream. I'd visit my Aunt Myrtle, who would pepper me with questions as to how we were all doing. That was the hard part. After that I could enjoy milk and cookies.

I tried smoking that summer. When Dad found out, he forced me to smoke several cigarettes in a row. I thought I was never going to be able to breathe again. Dad smoked, Mom had smoked; what was so wrong with me smoking? I still smoked on occasion but also carried SenSen breath mints to camouflage any telltale cigarette odor.

I wasn't seeing LeRoy as much. I "branched off" but it didn't always turn out well.

Bob, one of my classmates, asked if he could take me out. He was a smiley, fun-loving sort of guy. I said yes.

He had a car, which was appealing to me. We were driving around and soon he pulled off into a wooded area and parked the car. Almost immediately his lips were on mine and his hands were on my breast area. I broke away. "What are you doing?"

"I thought—,"

"Well, you thought wrong. Please take me home."

"I'm sorry, Rose. I really am."

Bob respected my request, but all I could think of was what kind of message was I sending, and what was being said about me.

Another time I wasn't so lucky. Camp Williams was an airbase, which helped the economy of our small town, but on the down side the base left many parents worried about their daughters being lured by the soldiers. But being naïve and trusting, I agreed to go out with one of those handsome guys in uniform. If I had been wise, I would have been suspicious when he didn't want to pick me up at my house but wanted me to meet him on a corner in town. I thought I was cool going out with someone with a car and to the city of Tomah, about twenty miles from Camp Douglas, to see the movie *Shane*.

As we drove to Tomah he mentioned how nice I looked, talked about the beautiful summer evening, and made me feel very comfortable. The business section of Tomah, including the theater, was on the main drag. When we reached the area of the theater, he continued driving and seemed to be heading out of town. With my head cranked and looking out the window I uttered, "We've passed the theater. You'll need to turn around."

He kept driving as though he hadn't heard me. "Where are we going?" I asked.

"For a ride."

"A ride? I thought we were going to the movie. We'll be late."

He drove, not paying attention to me. He was just staring ahead. Somehow I sensed I was in trouble. *Oh, dear God, please help me. I don't know what to do.*

I asked him to take me home, but he wasn't listening.

Several miles out of town the car slowed and he pulled off the road. It all happened so fast. The sound of him unzipping his trousers was deafening. He grabbed my hand, and tried placing it between his legs. Somehow I broke free and reached for the door handle, but he jerked me back by my ponytail. I thought he was going to yank it out of my head. He reached under my skirt, trying to pull my panties down. I fought and hit my knees on the dash.

"No, please don't do this!"

Still holding me by my hair, he took his hand out from under my skirt and hit me hard across the face. I tasted blood in my mouth.

Dear God, give me strength. If I'm going to die I'm going to die fighting.

I took my left fist and brought it down on his private parts. I felt his hand release my ponytail and, somehow in that split second, I managed to open the door, get out, and start running, running as fast as I could without looking back. *Please don't let anything happen to me. Who would ever think of looking for me in a cornfield?*

I tried listening for the sound of the car leaving, or footsteps, but all I heard was the thundering beat of my heart. The corn was not fully matured so I was taller than the corn. After running some distance, I lay face down between the rows. I was too frightened to stand up for fear he was looking for me. As I raised my head off the ground, I peered ahead at the long rows of corn, sentinels shielding me. I waited for darkness. It was so still with an occasional "caw-caw" from a crow. I could smell the soil. The taste of blood was in my mouth and with my tongue I felt a cut inside of my lip. I was thankful the evening air was warm as I lay there on the ground wearing a sleeveless blouse, skirt, and sandals. *How am I going to get home?*

It seemed to take forever for dusk to come. I needed to get help. I finally had the courage to stand up. I removed the rubber band from my ponytail, ran my fingers through my hair, and replaced the rubber band. I straightened my blouse and skirt and wiped off any field debris that might have been on my skirt. I couldn't see, but I am sure there was some. I started walking. *Please let me see a yard light or house light.* When I reached the end of the row I looked to the left, the right, and straight ahead, but nothing but darkness, so I turned and went back the other direction. I came to a fence bordering that end of the field, which gave me hope that I was near a farmhouse. Not knowing if the fence was electric, I slithered under the bottom wire. As I started walking I sensed that I was walking through a pasture because the surface was uneven. I hoped I would not step into a cow pie, but then it didn't matter because I saw the lights of a house.

I walked to the house but was scared to death to knock on the door. *What would I say? Would they call the police? Would they help me?* I knocked. The door opened. I suspect the woman of the house was more than surprised to see me on her doorstep. She looked younger than Mom. Thick braids encircled her head. Without taking her eyes off me she said, "John, there's a young girl at the door."

"Coming, Grace." *Grace—what a beautiful name.*

The man was tall, blonde, and had the typical farmer's tan: tan to the mid-forehead and then white where a hat would've protected his head.

"I'm sorry to bother you," I uttered, my mouth so dry I could barely speak,

He looked past me into the darkness. "Are you with someone? Has your car broken down?"

"No, I'm alone. Could I please bother you for a drink of water?"

"Yes, of course."

As I was standing there the light of the kitchen shone on my sandals and I noticed the end of my toes were dirty from lying down in the field. I quickly pulled them in as far as I could. I wondered what the rest of me looked like, and whether Grace noticed.

He returned with the glass of water. I gulped it down in seconds. "I really need a ride home—to Camp Douglas. I escaped from a bad situation."

Grace responded quickly, "Maybe we should call the police."

"Please don't. I don't even know the man's last name. I mean I was on a date. It just didn't turn out well. I think he's gone now. I just want to go home."

They looked at each other. I just wanted them to trust me and help me.

Grace spoke first, "I need to stay here as the baby is sleeping, but John, you'll drive her home, won't you?"

There seemed to be a communication between them without any spoken words. John reached for his cap and keys hanging on a wooden peg by the door. "I'll see you later, Grace."

I took a long look at the face of a woman I would never forget, an angel in the night.

We walked outside to a pick-up truck. As I climbed into the truck, I wished Grace were along but knew I had to trust her husband. I appreciated that no more questions were asked of me as he drove me home, except for directions and "I hope you'll be OK." I was also relieved when we passed through town, which meant we passed the police station. I hoped he hadn't heard me gasp a breath of relief.

I thanked him and, just as I was getting out of the truck, I said, "My name is Rose." I walked into the house and was relieved that everyone was in bed. The house was still warm from the day's heat. Supper odors hung in the air. A fly must have just got captured on the flypaper, evident by the distressful buzzing. "I'm home, Dad."

"OK, Rosie," Dad quickly responded from his bedroom. He must have been reading *or* waiting for me to get home.

I quietly removed my clothes and put them into the laundry basket, washed off my legs and arms, and crawled into bed. My sisters stirred in the darkness but quickly settled. The back of my head hurt. The night's events were spinning like a tornado in my mind.

Maybe I should have had John and Grace call the police, but would they have believed me? What would Dad's reaction have been? What if I see that soldier again? Dad knew I was going to a movie. Will he ask me about it? Will he be suspicious if I just say I liked it? Maybe he won't ask. I don't want to lie. Mom, life as a teenager is so complicated. I so wish you were here to put your arms around me. What would I have done without Grace and John? I just thank God for having angels in the most unlikely places.

I lay in bed trying to relax enough to fall asleep, but my tongue kept finding the cut in my mouth and I hoped I wouldn't have a bruise on the outside of my cheek when I woke up. Something was also telling me that I better be satisfied staying home and entertaining myself listening to radio shows like *Fibber McGee and Molly, The Great Gildersleeve, The Hit Parade,* or *Amos and Andy*—something safe.

I stayed close to home for the next few weeks. I didn't want to run into that soldier again. One Sunday after Mass I asked the priest if I could talk with him. I told my siblings to head home without me. The priest and I walked from the church to his house nearby. Once we went inside and into his office, I broke down almost immediately. "My child, my child. What's wrong?" I was used to talking to a priest behind a curtain in a confessional, not face to face. I felt so vulnerable and just wanted to leave. I wiped away tears with the tips of my fingers. "Everything seems to be going wrong and I don't think Mom is coming home again."

I remember Father sitting across from me at his desk, letting me pour out all my troubles—not all my troubles—I couldn't share my ordeal with the soldier. He leaned forward in his chair, looking right at me, "Rose, I'm sorry about your mom, your dad's drinking, and your growing pains, but you can get through this. I'm happy to see you at Mass each Sunday." He took my hand in his and said I needed to trust in God. And then he said something else I would never forget. He told me when I was struggling to think of the words from the song, *You'll Never Walk Alone.* Rogers and Hammerstein wrote this song for a musical. The words of the song I remember the most are: *When you walk, through a storm, hold your head up high and don't be afraid of the dark. You'll never walk alone.* The message of those lyrics helped me then as well as throughout my lifetime. I cannot thank my priest enough for that day in his office.

Chapter 13
Life is Not Static

The remaining summer went by quickly and soon it was time for school to start. There would only be two kids to worry about for childcare, as Barbara was starting first grade. I was happy for her because she was a smart, inquisitive, little girl and there would be structure in her life.

I was sad that my friend Barbara and her sisters and brother would not be attending Camp Douglas School but would be bused to Madonna Catholic School in Mauston.

With the start of fall there also was the start of squirrel season. Freddy was a regular Daniel Boone, except he didn't need a gun—he made do with a homemade slingshot. Susie loved tagging along with him. She was like a fly stuck on flypaper when it came to her brother.

I can still visualize the slain squirrel laid out on a board and Fred saying, "Sis, I can show you how to skin a squirrel." It was not my favorite learning experience. He demonstrated how to make a slit down the middle of the squirrel's back and then take hold of the skin and pull hard toward the tail. The skin peeled off the body. I would do the same on the other side, peeling back to the head and then cut the head off. Next he showed me how to make a slit down the belly and remove the innards. Lastly the skinned squirrel was rinsed thoroughly. The squirrel was cooked slowly in a pot of salted water with potatoes and carrots added later. If

I close my eyes and think back to that time, I can smell and taste the wildness of the meat, a flavor I particularly didn't like, but it was food on the table. I preferred the taste of rabbit, but they were a little harder to slay with a slingshot.

During the summer I met a girl named Shirley from a neighboring town, who often came to Camp Douglas to visit relatives. Shirley had short bobbed hair that showed off her natural curls. Her smile was infectious. She was flirty if any of the guys were around. She was cute and she knew it. They say opposites attract so I guess that is why I liked her.

She was in Camp Douglas on a weekend in October. She told me she would be staying overnight and a friend of hers would be picking her up on Monday morning. She suggested to me that I skip school and spend the day in Tomah with her.

"No, Shirley, I can't. My dad would kill me and besides I've never skipped school."

"Oh, come on, Rose. I bet you have good grades. One day won't hurt anything. We'll bring you back as the school day ends."

I couldn't believe I said yes. *What is it that drives a person to do something that in your heart you know is wrong? Was I craving attention?*

The next morning I walked to school as usual, even went into the building, and then walked back out and met Shirley and her friend. We drove to Tomah and tried not to be too conspicuous—truancy was a no-no. About noon, as we were walking down the main street to find a café, a police car slowed down and stopped at the curb. My heart raced when he asked if we were Shirley and Rose. *How would anyone know who we were? No one else knew our plan. We'd only been gone four hours.* I never did find out.

76

Shirley told the officer her friend would take us home, but that was not an option. The two of us were told to get in the police car, but not her friend. He was told to leave. I never did figure that one out. We were driven to the police station. As I sat on the hard wooden chair, I felt like I was going to throw up wondering how this would all turn out. Shirley was the quietest I'd ever seen. The officer returned from another room and informed us he was driving us home, but not without a lecture about the importance of school.

As we walked out of the station I noticed Shirley's friend parked across the street with a look of wonderment on his face. Shirley shrugged her shoulders and pointed to the police car. We got in and sat in silence. I thought about what Dad would say and already was feeling embarrassed about going to school in the morning. Shirley was dropped off first in the town of Oakdale. We arrived at my house at about two. The officer talked to Dad a few minutes and left. I was relieved that Patricia and Rita were taking their naps and that the others were not home from school yet. I just wanted Dad to yell at me and get it over with but he said nothing. That was the worst punishment ever. I knew he was disappointed in me. I went to my room.

The next day at school was difficult. The principal informed me that I wouldn't be able to volunteer in the office for the rest of the semester. I was told that any A's would be B's and any B's would be C's on my report card. I never skipped school again.

I still saw Barbara on weekends, but did meet a girl named Kathryn, who had moved from Kingston, Idaho, to Camp Douglas. Looking at her, it was as if she had no neck. She never seemed self-conscious about it—her personality wouldn't have allowed it. She loved to laugh and I always felt uplifted being in her presence. Kathryn and I enjoyed learning the words of the *Hit Parade* songs and singing them as we walked from each other's homes or just walking. Some of our favorites were: *Till I Waltz Again With You, Vaya con Dios, Doggie in the Window, Don't Let the Stars Get in Your Eyes,* and *Secret Love.*

It was through knowing Kathryn that I met a young man named Bill. She liked his brother Duane and they were from Tomah. Bill was not the most handsome guy in the world, but appeared to be a well-brought-up young man. He showed respect to my dad and took the time to speak to my brother and sisters. I knew the first time I met his parents why he was like he was. He came from a fun-loving home filled with laughter, *and* good food. This is how I thought our family would have been if Mom hadn't left. Bill's mother always took me aside when I was there and asked if there was anything she could do for me. When she found out I had a twelve-year-old brother, she offered clothes that her younger son had outgrown.

You may be wondering what became of LeRoy. LeRoy never left—he was a good friend I could tell my troubles to—he was always there when no one else was. He could give me a hug if I needed it. I couldn't tell him about the soldier incident, but I could tell him it was tough being a teenager and he understood.

My friend Barbara recounts a memory of hers on Halloween of 1953. We were going to meet at the Community Hall across from the church for a party put on by volunteers. It was always a fun time with the wearing of costumes, bobbing for apples, games, and plenty of treats. She said when I saw her coming up the street I began yelling, "I got it! I got it!" She said," You got what?"

"I got my period!"

Barbara was two years younger but already had gotten hers.

It was another time in my life when I wished Mom had been there. It was weird, especially then, to tell my dad and ask him for the money to buy what I needed. It was exciting and scary to know my body had the capacity to make a child.

*   *   *

I was on the homecoming court that school year, Mary Ann was in the spelling bee, and Barbara was picked to be a little flower girl for the First Communion ceremonies in the spring of 1954. Barbara looked so pretty thanks to one of the church ladies who somehow found some shoes and a white dress for her to wear.

I never lost hope for a letter from Mom. She just had to come home. One wintry afternoon I composed a letter to Mom, knowing it would not go anywhere except into my memory.

> Dear Mom, wherever you are, and I know you are somewhere, I feel it. The kids have grown so in the year and a half you've been gone. Little Patricia is like a cherub with her round face, big eyes, and beautiful smile. She is talking so much now. Rita looks more like you every day. When she cocks her head to the right and looks at me with those soulful eyes and smiles, my heart just melts. It's hard to correct her when she is doing something she shouldn't be. Barbie's hair is getting so long and pretty and is dark like yours. She always has her dolly with her. Dad took it away from her one day as a punishment and it was punishment of the worst kind for her. Susie is such a tomboy and wants to tag along with Freddie every chance she gets or I should say,

any chance Freddie gives her. She reminds me of a butterfly flitting in the wind. She has lost a couple of her baby teeth. Freddie is quite the marble champ—his collection is growing. He also is quite the squirrel hunter. Being a boy I think he has it harder than us girls. Dad isn't always the nicest to him. Mary has a good friend Vivian and loves going to her house to work on craft projects or riding Vivian's horse. Mary will be in the spelling bee this year and I will help her with her words like you did for me when I was in the competition. I know she'll do well. And me—what do I say about me? It would be much easier if you were here. I have so many questions. I have gone on a few dates and hope I am learning some life lessons along the way. I got my period a couple of months ago. I'm glad you and Dad had that conversation with me when I was fourteen. You discussed a lot more with me than they did in health class.

I was prom queen and I felt your presence in that dance hall. I know how much you and Dad enjoyed dancing.

Dad is doing the best he can under the circumstances. He doesn't say much but sometimes his drinking says it all.

Aunt Mabel and Aunt Myrtle drop in on a regular basis and bring care packages, usually groceries.

I'll never be the cook you were but I am learning little by little. One day Mary Ann surprised us with a cake she had baked. When we went to eat it something was not right. It was very dry. She said,"I followed all the directions except I didn't put in something called shortening. I didn't know what it was." She was only familiar with the word lard.

I don't know what will happen when I graduate. Right now we do the best we can day by day. I'm still waiting for your next letter or even better, you. You are in my prayers everyday hoping you are OK. Love your daughter, Rose

Chapter 14
Blessings in Disguise

It was in the spring of 1954. I fed the kids and myself supper. Dad was not home yet; then I heard, *"Mona Lisa, Mona Lisa..."* a beautiful song, but a song I only heard when Dad was very inebriated. I felt my body becoming tense and I wished I could've been elsewhere. I remember hoping he'd go straight to his room and to bed, even though I knew from experience it wouldn't happen. He'd want to talk and probably meant well, but when he was in that condition it felt like emotional abuse.

Dad staggered into the house, a smile on his face, "Hi, kiddies. Let me fix you supper." I could smell his breath as soon as he walked in the door—such a rotten odor.

"We ate already," I said.

Mary had a special connection with Dad, and offered to get him something. "No, no, that's OK," he answered as he steadied himself with one hand on the corner of the table.

Freddy stayed in the background, as Dad often singled him out, saying, "You want to learn to fight? Come on, put up your dukes." Dad would hold up his fists and Freddy would back up and say, "I don't want to fight, Dad."

The little ones stayed close to me.

I sighed a breath of relief when Dad maneuvered himself into the living room and plopped down in the easy chair, his arm loosely draped over the arm rest, legs stretched out, and soon we heard his back-of-the-throat snoring. He didn't stay awake long enough to remove his cowboy boots.

My sense of relief turned to fear when I couldn't arouse him to tell him to go to bed. I tried and tried and then became frightened. *Could someone die from drinking?* I had one of the kids run across the street to the Humphrey house and get help. Mr. and Mrs. Humphrey were older folks whom I'm sure wondered how and if we were managing. They both came over and assured us Dad would be OK in the morning. I wasn't so sure but I had to hope they knew what they were talking about.

*   *   *

In the spring of my junior year, driving lessons were given as part of the curriculum at school. I was excited, but at the same time, wondered what good it would do, as Dad didn't own a car. Would I remember what I learned when and if I had the opportunity to drive?

I did get a chance to drive in June. My friend Kathy and I, and a friend of hers who had a car, were coming home from Tomah one evening.

"Bob, I have my license. Could I drive the rest of the way home?"

"Sure, but let's go to Camp Douglas by taking the county road. There will be little or no traffic."

We turned off Highway 16 at Oakdale, an unincorporated village between Tomah and Camp Douglas. Bob pulled over and we exchanged sitting positions. All three of us were in the front seat, Bob in the middle, and Kathy by the window. I was cautious at first, thinking about the position of the gas and brake pedal, hand signals, speed, and driving in the dark, but after one or two miles my comfort increased, and then… I was going the speed limit, but it was too fast for the hairpin curve staring me in the face. Before I could react, forces beyond my control had taken over. I felt my body being pushed against Bob as the car flipped over. It felt like a wild carnival ride, without the midway music. I heard screams; probably mine. We stopped with a thud; my hands had a death grip on the steering wheel. The car was upright but the steering wheel was pushed into my abdomen, making me a prisoner in my seat. I peered through the windshield that looked more like a spider web, and was chilled by the eeriness of the headlights casting their beacon on emerging corn shoots. I was brought back to reality by the pressure of Bob's head resting on my shoulder, and by his moans.

"Bob, are you all right?" I asked in a breathy voice. Before he had a chance to answer, I noticed Kathy was not in the car, and worse, there was no passenger door. *Dear God, help us!*

I painfully managed to wiggle free of the steering wheel, and tried opening the door. It was jammed. As Bob exited on the passenger side he clutched his side and uttered, "I think I have broken ribs." I slid across the seat, stepped out of the car into the cornfield, and yelled, "Kathy, where are you? Please answer me." I ran, continuing to call her name, and then I bumped into something—it was Kathy. She was on her back, and seemed lifeless. "Bob, she's over here." I turned my head and vomited. And then I heard, "My neck. My neck."

"Rose, stay by her. I'm going to a farmhouse and get help."

There I was, in another cornfield, in the dark, praying that Kathy wouldn't die, and that Bob would find another John and Grace without collapsing with his own injuries. *When you walk through a storm, hold your head up high, and don't be afraid of the dark.*

It seemed hours before I saw headlights shining into the field. Bob, along with two police officers, walked toward us carrying a large flashlight and a stretcher. "We're over here," I nervously called out.

"Kathy, someone's here to help us," I whispered in her ear. "Please forgive me." They checked Kathy, loaded her on the stretcher, and took the three of us to Tomah Hospital. X-rays confirmed a small neck fracture on Kathy. The fracture was less of a problem than trying to fit her with a neck brace, due to her neck deformity. Bob did have a couple of broken ribs, and I was told to report any persistent abdominal discomfort or vomiting. I don't believe the vomiting episode was caused by a concussion; I was just so afraid.

We all healed, but I would not drive again until I was 28 years old.

*   *   *

On July 16, 1954, Dad was served a summons to appear at the Mauston Courthouse at 2p.m. on July 21. I'm sure this was because of concern by well-meaning neighbors, clergy, or school staff. I never knew the source. The charge was neglect. How could they call it neglect? Love isn't neglect. Trying as hard as you can isn't neglect. Mom said God would take care of us because we were good. *Well, maybe He is taking care of us. I have to believe that.*

Dad and the seven of us walked up the courthouse sidewalk. The sun was shining but it felt like a black cloud was hanging over us. I was remembering happier times when we lived in Mauston, and Mom and Dad would bring us here to visit Santa Claus and get a bag of candy.

What happens when a parent is charged with neglect? Maybe Dad and I will just get a talking-to, telling us we have to come up with a new plan. Maybe Dad will have to find a live-in housekeeper, even though he tried that once or twice since Mom left. It won't be easy.

We walked into the courtroom. Our footsteps sounded loud, but not as loud as I imagined my heartbeat to be. My sisters and brother looked frightened, my dad worried. I just wanted to be back in Camp Douglas, at the swimming hole, anywhere besides the courtroom. A woman approached and talked with my dad for a few minutes. She wore a tailored suit, but I noticed her blouse had lacy detail. She appeared to be caring as she stooped down to be at my little sisters' level to speak with them. I could tell she liked us. She told us she was a social worker.

We were seated on a long wooden bench. As I sat, nervously waiting, my fingers were aware of ridges, like a washboard, along the armrest—I touched them, I counted them, I hoped I wouldn't touch someone's gum, but then I thought, people only leave their gum on bedposts to save for the next day, making sure any metal was removed that might have come off the bedpost. *Maybe no one else saved his or her gum for the next day.*

My thoughts were interrupted by footsteps, very determined footsteps. It was the judge in his black robe entering the courtroom. He walked confidently and sat down without much expression on his face, just staring down at the social worker and us. He addressed my dad about the neglect charges, but then there was the unexpected. I heard the judge say it was in our best interest to be placed at St. Michael's Orphanage in La Crosse, Wisconsin, until foster home placement could be arranged. *But we are not orphans— we have a father. What about giving us a chance?* I heard Ms. Jelen, the social worker, asking the judge if after the initial time at the orphanage, she could place all of us in foster homes within La Crosse.

The judge answered in an *I know it all* voice, "That will never happen. You are going to have to find homes no matter where they are in the state."

Ms. Jelen persisted. "But, Your Honor, I would like to try. My first impression of this family is that they are very close."

The judge nodded without enthusiasm. I wondered if all judges were as cold as he appeared.

I have no recall of how we got to the orphanage that day. My brother recalls there were two cars driven by orphanage staff, which means to me that all this had been decided before we ever got to court. I do know we didn't have a chance to say goodbye to our friends. We did stop at the house to gather up a few things. I took my photo album, my camera, which was my eyes and recorder of history, and a pair of earrings and a bracelet, which had been my mom's. Freddy asked the social worker about Pepper, our dog, and Inky, our cat. When Freddy heard her say we would have to leave the pets behind with Dad, he bolted for the nearby woods screaming, "If they can't come, I'm not going either." A miracle happened when they told him he could bring them along.

Dad seemed a broken man as we tearfully said our goodbyes. He lost his wife and now us, in a way. My fear was his drinking would increase.

I'd never been to La Crosse, which was about an hour away from Camp Douglas. The long driveway on the orphanage property was lined by mature trees and ended with a circular drive. What I could see of the grounds looked beautiful. We would find out later, during our orientation, that a tributary of the Mississippi River flowed behind the orphanage, a place where we could swim and canoe if desired. When I got out of the car, the massive, three-story stone building loomed before me. Ms. Jelen led us up the entrance stairs, through heavy wooden doors, into the place that was to be home.

As the head nun greeted us, I wondered how many other children she had welcomed to this place. In my mind I knew this was probably for the best, but I was not prepared for the division of "my family." After a brief orientation, the supervising nuns of each group came to take us to our respective living quarters. Patricia, Rita, and Barbara were assigned to the babies' section, Susan to the young girls, Fred to the boys' wing, and Mary and I to the older girls' area. Patricia, Rita, and Barbara clung to me. "We want to stay by you, Rosie."

"It'll be OK. I'll come and see you as soon as I can." The social worker placed her hand on my shoulder and gave it a gentle squeeze.

The nun assigned to the Sodality girls, the group I was in, stood tall and erect with authority. She led me to the community closet and instructed me to pick out some clothing. As I moved clothes on hangers this way and that, looking for something I might like, I heard, "You're taking too long. Don't be so choosy." *One day I'm making decisions along with Dad and now I sense someone will be making decisions for me. Freedom was slipping away and I didn't like it.* She added, "I'll be giving you name labels to sew into your clothes." I held back tears as best I could.

I didn't sleep much the first night. Questions were pelting my brain like a hailstorm. *How are my brother and sisters doing? If Patricia has to go potty, will there be someone to take her? Did Freddy get a chance to say goodnight to Pepper, wherever he is? Pepper will be so confused, as well as Inky. We* learned the next day that all the animals stayed in a barn on the property.

How is Dad coping? What about my friends? Will I ever see them again? I shared with my best friend, Barbara, about the summons, but neither of us suspected this would happen. What will the teachers think when I'm not there in September? I'd already been told at the end of my junior year I would be valedictorian or salutatorian of the senior class.

The unknown was scary. I hoped Ms. Jelen was right about her plan to find homes in the La Crosse area. I vowed no matter what happened I would *not* allow us to lose track of one another, never, never, never.

I closed my eyes, hoping the breathing of my seven roommates would lull me to sleep.

*   *   *

The structure of the orphanage, both physically and emotionally, swallowed me up: the long hallways, the many-stalled bathrooms, the high-ceilinged dormitories with beds and upright closets along both sides of the room. The dining room was filled with long tables, and the kitchen area had large-scale appliances such as the potato masher and mix master, which were taller than I. The refrigerators and freezers had floor-to-ceiling doors, the ovens were massive, and the sinks large enough to accommodate the washing of over-sized pots and pans. The dishwasher was a steaming monster with two mouths. Dishes were put into large trays and transported into the *first mouth* by moving rollers. The door would shut and when the dishes were clean the, *other mouth* opened, steam poured out and the trays exited on another set of rollers. I used to compare myself to the dishes, wondering how I would emerge.

While in the orphanage, age-appropriate assignments were given. We "older" residents helped in the kitchen and dining room. Washing pots and pans was my least favorite chore, especially in August, without air conditioning, wearing rubberized aprons, and scrubbing enormous pots in deep sinks. I'd be happy when the different groups marched into the dining room and I could get a glimpse of my brother and sisters and give a little wave and throw a kiss. We couldn't eat as a family.

I considered the laundry building my first sauna. It was unbelievably hot and humid. I can close my eyes and smell "that smell," a combination of industrial soap, heat, and plenty of perspiration. Ironing boards were in a row. If you were older, you ironed, and if younger, you may have been folding towels and washcloths or items that didn't need ironing. On the upside, it was a great place for socializing, although the nun supervisor might have called it something else.

My favorite assignment was setting up the nuns' dining room. Even opening the door was a visual experience. The carpeted room was of normal size, with a dark wooden china hutch and dining room table. Absent was the echo you heard when walking the wood floors of the hallways and dormitories. Beautiful china, silverware, and stemware graced the ivory colored linen tablecloth. It was in this dining room where I had my first sip of wine. Sister Julaine, one of my favorite nuns, was telling Jeanette, another resident, and me to observe the china and silverware placement. I learned to remember on which side of the plate the silverware should be placed—*spoon, knife*, and the word *right* have five letters each, and the words *fork* and *left* have four letters each. Over the years, I have repeated those words to my children and grandchildren.

It was when Sister was telling us about the wine that she asked if we wanted a taste. She probably could have gotten in trouble since we were only seventeen, but it was much more than just giving us a taste of wine. It was warmth, caring, and her showing a human side, having us imagine for a few minutes that we were in the dining room of someone's home, and not in an institution.

The orphanage did become *home*. I was given the choice of being in a foster home or not. Since I was going to be a senior and if by some miracle a college student post-graduation—I chose not to go into a foster home—a decision I sometimes regretted since I didn't have a place to hang my hat. Dad eventually moved in with his sister Mabel in New Lisbon, so when I could, I visited. Mary was placed into a home March 1955; Barbara and Rita went as a pair also in 1955: Patricia would not be placed for four years; and Susan was a resident of St. Michael's six years before placement. Fred was the only one who was in a home outside of La Crosse because of his request to be on a farm. He actually was in two different homes, the first one being with abusive foster parents in 1956. He rode his bike from Ettrick back to the orphanage, a distance of thirty miles, to escape that situation, and was placed with a loving family about a year later.

I often wondered what were the first impressions of the seven of us, ages five to seventeen, the day of our arrival. In preparation for this memoir, I was pleased to read in orphanage records the following: *There is an impression that there must have been much love and many strengths in this family which gave the children enough security to move into an institutional placement a little more easily than might be expected.*

Chapter 15
Transitions

The weeks following our admission to St. Michael's were filled with orientation, and registration for age-appropriate Catholic schools.

My school would be Aquinas High School. I had seven classmates in Camp Douglas; now I would have 213. One of my electives was Latin, a requirement for nursing school. I wasn't giving up hope of continuing my education.

School began the day after Labor Day, and I was nervous. How would I be accepted coming from the orphanage? Usually by the time one is a senior, you know your classmates well. I would only be familiar with others from the home. Sister Julaine drove us the several blocks to Aquinas. We'd be walking thereafter, except in inclement weather. I felt proper in my navy blue skirt and white blouse, which was the required dress code. Navy blue sweaters were permissible during cool weather. With the limited selection of clothing at the orphanage, I was grateful for uniforms. After a few weeks at school, I did notice subtle differences between the wealthy and not-so-wealthy students' uniforms; wool versus cashmere, plain collars versus appliquéd or lace-trimmed collars, but it was OK. It was the person in the uniform that mattered.

I got out of the station wagon, turned, thanked Sister Julaine for the ride, and paused a moment at the curb. The massive three-story, red brick structure loomed before me.

I observed other students arriving and displaying excitement: hugs, hellos, and waves as they saw familiar faces. I felt a pang of envy.

I remember walking into school, butterflies in my stomach in an absolute frenzy, and saying to myself, *I can do this*. I would soon learn that Aquinas High School was a special place, where I felt accepted by the nuns, priests, and fellow students.

My senior subjects were bookkeeping, Latin, English, chemistry, religion, and civics. Since I'd never had Latin before, I was assigned to the freshman Latin class, and was like a "big sister" to the underclassmen. My final exam earned me a *Magna cum laude* (with great praise) certificate.

I wasn't able to attend all activities at Aquinas, but was pleased I could go to the football games and school plays. A very special event was a retreat, which I had never experienced. I thought it amazing when things showed up in your life when you needed it the most. Father Ireland, the retreat master, talked on relationships, marriage, and some of the sadness he had observed in homes and prisons. I left that retreat knowing I was not the only person with problems, and wanting to do more for Christ.

*   *   *

I would be at the orphanage for ten and a half months. My routine was school, orphanage chores (some of which we were paid for), visiting my brother and sisters as often as possible in the orphanage and foster home setting; and writing informative letters to Dad. I also responded to letters from several of my aunts, who kept in touch on a regular basis.

I almost lost my paying job in the orphanage clinic because the nun thought I was not spending my money wisely. She thought I was spending it foolishly on clothing and cigarettes. I didn't know this bit of information until I was reading those letters my dad had saved. Sister had written an addendum at the bottom of one of my letters to Dad. I did smoke occasionally, but I certainly did not earn enough money to spend it foolishly.

I visited Patricia and Susan when they were patients at St. Francis Hospital, having tonsillectomies, Susan in November 1954, and Patricia in March 1955. I was aware of the antiseptic scent as I entered the hospital. I observed the polished floors of the long hallways, and nurses wearing white uniforms and starched white caps, quietly going in and out of patient's rooms. This is how I visualized a hospital setting, having read *Cherry Ames: Student Nurse* by Helen Wells. *This is what I want to do. I want to take care of others.*

The orphanage staff did their best to give us a chance to see family and have experiences in the community. Mary and I were able to go by Greyhound bus to spend Christmas of 1954 with Aunt Mabel and Dad. My Aunt Cecile and Uncle John sent a dollar for each of us kids that Christmas. On New Year's Day, movies for children were shown in the local theater, and every resident had the opportunity to go. I took responsibility for Patricia, Rita, Barbara, and Susan. There were ten cartoons and a Three Stooges movie. They were so excited to be in a real theater since they had only seen outdoor street movies in Camp Douglas.

The outdoor street movies came up another time. A movie was shown at the orphanage called, *Five Little Peppers in Trouble*. Eight-year-old Barbara said to her group mother, "I saw that movie at our free shows on Saturday nights." Did I ever laugh; it was so cute the way she said it!

On another occasion Sister Julaine transported several of us teenagers to the Westby Ski Jump competition. Westby was a small community thirty miles from St. Michael's. I'd never witnessed anyone on skis, speeding down an almost-vertical structure, catapulting into the air, and landing 210 feet away; the record at the time was 219 feet. Were the competitors brave or irrational? —You tell me.

*   *   *

Helen was a lay worker who was employed and assigned to the kitchen. Helen and I hit it off with one another, like a mother-daughter relationship. She lived a few blocks from the orphanage and received permission to take me off grounds for short visits or a meal at her home. I enjoyed the change of scenery.

In the early months of 1955, when foster home placement was taking place for three of my sisters, I made frequent visits to the social services office located on the grounds of the orphanage. *Would I be able to visit them and how often? Could we celebrate birthdays and other special occasions?* I was pleased when Mary Ann's foster parents, Margaret Mary and Larry, had a surprise fifteenth birthday party for her, and the rest of us were invited.

My siblings and I were able to attend Barbara and Rita's First Communion day held at St. Thomas Moore Church, Barbara in 1955, and Rita in 1956.

Dad corresponded with me about twice a month, sometimes more. He was conscientious about sending Valentine cards, Easter cards, and remembering our birthdays. He visited when time off permitted and when rides were available, which was not often. I was always happy to see him, but was sad when he shared the fact he didn't feel well received by Barbara and Rita's foster parents; sometimes Dad could see the kids through the front door, but Mrs. Senn would not acknowledge him. Dad learned to arrange the accompaniment of a social worker when he visited. I can't say for sure, but maybe Mrs. Senn was worried that the girls would be emotionally traumatized at seeing Dad and not being able to go with him.

The foster parents required Barbara and Rita to assume the last name of Senn, and not Steinmetz. I wondered about the legality of it since they were not adopted.

I missed my friend Barbara, as well as others in Camp Douglas. I kept up correspondence with several of my friends and Mrs. Birkeness (Aunt Irene). LeRoy came to visit once, but further visits were discouraged. I don't know for sure, but I don't think the nuns wanted the worry of male/female relationships.

My closest friends in the orphanage setting were three girls my age: Mary, Rosalie, and Jeanette. One day we were given permission to take a canoe ride on the tributary of the Mississippi River, which flowed behind the orphanage. We were instructed to return by three in the afternoon. It was a beautiful day. The autumn leaves were brilliant, casting rainbow hues on the calm water. Sounds of honking geese and quacking ducks could be heard. The paddles provided a rhythm all their own as they dipped in and out of the water, droplets glistening in the sunshine.

The afternoon was mesmerizing, so mesmerizing we paddled farther than we should have. The three of us knew we wouldn't get back on time and suspected we'd be met on the shore by our superiors', handing out the verdict of no canoe privileges for the rest of the fall season. We came to shore, tethered the canoe, pretended to look very sad when we received our punishment, and headed up the bank. Once out of our superior's sight, we smiled. We had blisters on our hands and didn't want to paddle a canoe anytime soon.

Chapter 16
Dreams Do Come True

I was shy but assertive when I was passionate about something, such as wanting to be a nurse. I mentioned my desires to the social worker and she assured me I would be able to go on to school. Likewise, a well-dressed woman came to the orphanage, introduced herself as Mrs. Hilton, and was asking us senior girls what our goals and aspirations were. Again, I talked about my wish to be a nurse. Sensing a glimmer of hope, I applied to the School of Nursing in La Crosse in March of 1955, and took the pre-entrance exam on April 30, 1955, meeting the requirements.

I'll never forget the day in May I came home from school and was told by Sister Bertina that I would be going to the Hotel Stoddard in La Crosse after supper.

"The Hotel Stoddard? Why there?"

"It's a surprise. Put on some nice clothes. One of the nuns will drive you there. Be ready at 6:30 p.m."

As I ate supper, I racked my brain trying to figure out why *I* was going, and no one else. The Hotel Stoddard was the social center of the city, but not for someone living in an orphanage.

Sister dropped me off, informing me she'd be back to pick me up. Hotel personnel directed me to a large meeting room. The size of the room was overwhelming, as well as the crystal chandeliers. As I glanced around the room, I observed other people my age, and a group of distinguished-looking ladies. One of the women approached me and introduced herself as Mrs. Morley. She had a warm smile, and made me feel less nervous. As she showed me to my place at a highly polished, long wooden table, I saw one of my classmates, causing me to be even more puzzled as to why I was there. I sat stiffly, hands on my lap, aware of underarm perspiration.

"Welcome. I am Mrs. Morley and represent the Zonta Women's Club, a club of business women. We are here this evening, along with other organizations, to award scholarships to deserving students."

Scholarships. Did I hear her say scholarships? Tears filled my eyes. My heart beat so hard I wondered if the person seated next to me could hear it.

The sound of clapping brought me back to attention. A student had been awarded a scholarship. Then I heard my classmate Ruth Stellpflug's name. She was awarded a one-year scholarship to St. Francis School of Nursing. I peered down to the end of the table where she was seated, made eye contact, and smiled.

Mrs. Morley stood at the podium. "The next recipient is Rose Steinmetz. Rose, you are the first winner of the Loretta Morley Nursing Scholarship, which will cover your entire three-year course at St. Francis School of Nursing."

I stood up, stunned and appreciative. "Thank you so much." As people clapped, I wondered who was responsible for this honor. Was it Ms. Jelen, the social worker; Mrs. Hilton who visited us at the orphanage; or was it Sister Cecile, my bookkeeping teacher, who questioned me about my plans for the future?

When I returned to St. Michael's, I sat down and wrote a letter to Dad and told him I would have a surprise when he came for my graduation. I wanted to tell him in person. I also had my conversation with Mom: *Mom, I remember you telling me how you would have liked to have been a nurse. I'm getting that chance against all odds. I will strive to become the best nurse possible.*

Chapter 17
Post High School Graduation

Igraduated from Aquinas High School June 5, 1955, in the top third of my class. Because of the size of our class, our graduation ceremony was held in a most unlikely setting, the newly built seminary on the outskirts of La Crosse. Dad attended and gifted me with money, and more important, his pride in me.

Graduation Day was officially my last day at St. Michael's Home, (the term "orphanage" had been replaced by "home" because it was rare to have an orphan reside there) but I would return for one overnight stay prior to the day of my nursing school registration.

After the ceremony, I tearfully said goodbye to Freddy, Susan, and Patricia, assuring them I would keep in touch, and then loaded my belongings into the wood-sided station wagon of Mr. O'Brien, my friend Jeanette's dad. The kids were so pleased to see Dad. Mr. O'Brien then drove us over to see Barbara, Rita, and Mary Ann in their respective foster homes. I know it was a day of mixed emotions for Dad, first the excitement of my graduation, and then his happiness of seeing everyone clouded over by having to leave.

We dropped Dad off in New Lisbon, along with items I would not be using during the summer or at the dormitory in the fall. It was good seeing Aunt Mabel, as I hadn't seen her for a while.

Jeanette, her dad, and I went on to Milwaukee where we boarded the *Milwaukee Clipper*, a boat that carried tourists and cars, and navigated across Lake Michigan to Manistee, Michigan. It was an all-night excursion, and exciting for two eighteen-year-olds who had never experienced anything like it before. There was a dancing lounge complete with an orchestra. I don't remember sleeping at all that night.

Upon our return, we drove to a South Milwaukee suburb and stayed at a relative of Mr. O'Brien's for two days. Although Jeanette and I would take a stroll only a few blocks from her relative's home, we felt like big city girls.

On June 8, Jeanette and I arrived in Lyndon Station, Wisconsin, where we'd be employed for three months, working in a tourist café called Christy's, and living in the company of the owners, Christy and Warren Bruns, our designated foster parents for the summer. We hadn't met them previously so we were apprehensive, but not for long. They welcomed us with outstretched arms, and smiles.

Christy and Warren looked to be in their thirties, and had an energetic six-year-old daughter named Paulette. I was pleased they had a daughter. It would ease the pain of being away from my siblings. Christy was petite, had a ready smile, and appeared to be nurturing and attentive. She spoke with an accent. I would learn she was born in Belgium and spoke French as well as English. Warren was tall and strikingly handsome, with dark hair, a ready smile, and great presence.

After we said goodbye to Jeanette's dad we were familiarized with the family living quarters, which were on the second floor over the restaurant. Jeanette and I would share a bedroom. When I went to bed that night, I knew I was in a good place for the summer.

The next day Jeanette and I were given a thorough orientation of the restaurant. We were taught how to operate the cash register; we reviewed the menu, learned how to make malts, and were coached on waitress etiquette. We were introduced to Millie, who worked in the kitchen. Millie was the sort of person that anyone would want for a mother, aunt, or friend. She had a quiet manner and an aura of love and kindness.

I thought our uniforms were perky looking. They were pink nylon with black trim and had a matching apron. Our shifts were 5 a.m. to 1 p.m. and 7 a.m. to 2:30 p.m. Jeanette worked one shift and I worked the other and we'd switch every week. The restaurant's specialties were great breakfasts and seafood lunches. Christy and Warren's café was unique for being in a town of less than four hundred residents. The walls were graced by fine art, and it was here I learned of Van Gogh. Christy had grown up with an appreciation of art as her father had been an artist in Belgium, and had the distinction of being commissioned to do a portrait of a king. A self-portrait of her father hung on the wall.

Lyndon Station was a small community, not many miles from Wisconsin Dells, a tourist destination. This little town had a church, grocery store, a motel at the west end of town, several bars, a post office, another restaurant called Martha's, and a filling station located next to the café. Jeanette and I would get to know the owners of the station by the end of the summer, as George and Mike were regular breakfast customers. I would get to know Martha as well. Her restaurant catered to more of the local folk, and was open in the evening, while Christy's served mainly tourists. The teenagers in town liked hanging out there, respecting Martha's standards of good behavior.

I learned a great deal about the importance of good customer relations and restaurant cleanliness. Warren held us to the highest of standards. When customers were finished with their meals and had left, we were required to wipe off the table, salt and pepper shakers, and ketchup and mustard containers, even if they hadn't been touched.

My salary was $21 a week, which Warren held onto until the end of summer and paid as a lump sum. My tips were my spending money.

One day while working, a handsome, dark-haired young man came into the café. There was an immediate attraction, and I barely concentrated on taking his order. Perez Prado's song, *Cherry Pink and Apple Blossom White*, playing on the jukebox, enhanced the moment. I learned his name was Wayne and he lived a few blocks away, of course in Lyndon everything was only a few blocks away. He showed up every day about the same time, but any conversations we had happened as I brought his order to him. Warren didn't approve of any dilly-dallying around. On about the fifth day, Wayne asked for a date. I wanted to say yes on the spot, but because Warren was strict and held Jeanette and me to a curfew, I had to tell Wayne I needed to first talk to Warren and Christy.

Our dates would be going swimming on my day off, chatting in the back yard, or hanging out with others from the area. One evening we had a date with the directive to be home by nine o'clock. Warren must have been on guard duty, because as Wayne and I were standing at the base of the wooden, outdoor stairway leading to the upstairs living quarters, with our lips pursed for a goodnight kiss, we were stopped in our tracks by Warren's lilting voice, "Time to say goodnight." And when I got upstairs Warren gave me parental advice about not being too generous with my kisses. *I wondered to myself if Warren knew how a girl gets all warm and tingly inside—of course, he knew. He had a wife and a daughter. He was watching out for me.*

I really missed my brother and sisters and wrote frequently. Shortly after I started working, I sent postcards to all my sibs. Sister Fabian, Patricia's group mother, sent me a letter telling me how happy Patricia was with her card: *She was so happy with her card you should see it, it's so worn out you can hardly tell it was a card. Patricia said I should tell you that she is a good girl, and you should come and see her. There is nobody like Rosie.*

I was pleased when it was necessary for me to take a Greyhound bus to La Crosse in July to have the nursing pre-entrance physical and dental examination, and the chance to make a short visit to see Susan, Fred, and Patricia. It seemed they had grown inches since I last saw them. Saying goodbye was the hardest. I wasn't able to see Barbara and Rita as they were at a Girl Scout camp with their foster sisters, Cathy and Lenore, and their foster mom, who was a Girl Scout leader. My sister Mary came back with me and spent a couple of days. I couldn't thank Christy and Warren enough for being so gracious. Mary returned for another visit at the end of July, and Barbara and Rita and their family surprised me with a visit on their way to Wisconsin Dells for vacation.

I turned eighteen that summer and Christy and Warren made sure it was a special day for me. We went to Wisconsin Dells to see the Tommy Bartlett Water Ski Show, a show still very popular today. Late that afternoon, Jeanette and I went with Wayne and friends, Carol and Jerry, to watch a donkey baseball game. Just imagine playing baseball while sitting on a donkey, hitting the baseball, and not being able to get to first base because of a stubborn donkey. I laughed until my sides hurt. Afterwards we went to the café, had cake and ice cream, and I opened gifts and cards. Going to a dance in the area was a wonderful ending to the day. It was wonderful because as I danced with Wayne, I knew I was falling in love.

Mom, life can be so complicated. I've met someone I really, really like. His name is Wayne. I will be starting my nurse's training in September and Wayne is thinking seriously of joining the Air Force. You would probably say it is for the best if he goes into the service so I can concentrate on my studies, but I know I will miss him a lot. Wayne has two brothers, Bud and Carl, and a sister, Rosalie. His dad has a serious nature, but his mom, Gladys, is personality plus. She has a wonderful sense of humor, really enjoys life, is a great cook, and I do think she likes me.

I know you know I turned eighteen today. I guess I'm officially an adult, but I have so much to learn. Wish you were here to help me out. I love you and miss you and hope you are OK. Goodnight Mom.

The three months at Christy's Café passed by quickly and it was time to return to La Crosse. It was to my advantage getting the lump sum payment of about $250.00 from Warren. I used some of the money to buy a watch with a second hand, (which was required for taking pulses), white shoes, and bandage scissors.

Wayne joined the Air Force in August, and left Lyndon Station a week before I did. It was difficult to see him go. I'd miss hearing him call me "Squirt," and the way he said it. I'd miss the ease of how we could talk and laugh together. We considered ourselves as going steady and promised to write. An open invitation from his mom to come and stay at her house anytime I had time off, including bringing a friend or family member, was comforting.

Christy, Warren, and Paulette drove us to our destinations. Jeanette went to Black River Falls, a community about halfway between Lyndon Station and La Crosse, but first we stopped in New Lisbon so I could see Dad. Both he and my Aunt Mabel wished me the very best in nursing school. The last stop was returning me to St. Michael's Home. Tears were shed and hugs exchanged, and I knew Christy, Warren, and Paulette had become much more than just a summer family and were in my life to stay.

Walking back into St. Michael's felt a little bit like home because of the welcome from the nuns and a few of my roommates. I noticed some new arrivals and wondered to myself about their situation and how they were coping. I visited Fred, Susan, and Patricia as soon as I was able but had to tell them I'd be leaving the next day for school. They knew I'd visit as often as possible.

As I settled in the orphanage dormitory bed for the last time, my thoughts of all that had transpired over the past year filled my head. I remembered the seven of us huddled together in the foyer of the orphanage, not sure of what was to come. I didn't like being seventeen and having a more restrictive life, and it took some adjustment to having nuns for *parents*. Three of my sibs had to make the transition into foster homes; the other three had to wonder when they would go into a home. We all survived going to schools with large enrollments. I communicated with Dad through letters, keeping him informed the best I could about the kids and myself. I thought about Wayne, but my last thought before going to sleep that night was anticipation of the soon-to-start next chapter of my life.

Chapter 18
Nursing School, Etcetera

ugust 31, 1955
I entered the building realizing that St. Francis School of Nursing was not only my place of continued education but my home for the next three years. Parents were milling about, giving last-minute advice to their daughters, some who were teary, and other parents were helping carry in belongings. I felt lonely and on the outside of the circle. *I told myself to quit feeling sorry for myself. I was not the only girl in the world without a mother, but at that moment, I felt like the only girl in the world without a mother.*

It pleased me when I saw several of my classmates from Aquinas. A familiar face was a good thing at that moment.

A brief orientation held in the lobby instructed parents and students regarding room assignments, home visitation, and numbers to call in case of an emergency. We were told we were expected to attend Mass each day in the hospital chapel. A buzzer in the dorm would wake us at 5:15 a.m. and Mass started at 5:50 a.m.

Our rooms had a bed, a metal dresser and desk, as well as a closet. We were able to personalize our rooms with bedspreads of our choosing. There was a community bathroom with toilets, sinks, bathtubs, and showers. Our meals would be served in the hospital cafeteria.

Our superiors were Sister Francita, Director of Nursing, and Sister Mary Aquin, Assistant Director. As one entered the school there was a reception desk. The lady behind the desk, Irene Mairich, was an important figure in the life of the nursing student. She was the first person you saw as you entered the building and the last one as you left.

One of the first things we were required to do was go to the sewing room, wearing our nursing uniform, and be measured. All uniforms had to be twelve inches from the bottom of the hem to the floor.

We received our woolen nursing capes, which were to be worn during cold weather to walk to Viterbo College for classes in anatomy, microbiology, chemistry, psychology, and sociology.

The laundry room in the basement was equipped with a couple of washers and dryers and an ironing board. Some students never saw the laundry room in three years because their parents did their laundry. They will never know all the fun they missed. The laundry room was a student confessional of sorts.

I was officially presented with my $500 scholarship on Thursday, September 1, 1955, a day after registering at school, with a *La Crosse Tribune* photographer present. It was special, because a few months before I didn't know how I'd be able to finance ongoing education. I wished my parents could have been spectators for an important time in my life. Transportation was always an obstacle for Dad, but I knew he was there in thought.

I missed seeing my siblings as often, but by January of 1956, I had a schedule worked out. Every Wednesday I'd visit Barbara and Rita at their foster home and on weekends, I'd visit Susan, Patricia, and Fred at St. Michael's Home. This schedule fluctuated depending on my hospital assignments, but it was workable. Mary Ann, and I would get together for a movie or I'd visit her at the Alland's (her foster parents). On occasion I spent the weekend with her, and Mrs. Alland made me feel most welcome. She insisted I call her by her first name, Margaret Mary. I really enjoyed sitting down in a cozy dining room to a home-cooked meal. I appreciated Margaret Mary giving me tasks to do, such as helping set the table or assisting with meal preparation. It gave me a sense of family.

The nursing school had a babysitting service. Parents in the community were able to call the school and request a sitter. A chart posted at the front desk listed opportunities for babysitting and we could accept jobs as our schedules permitted. The parents provided the transportation. If a family really liked you they'd ask if you were available. Babysitting, which paid 25 cents an hour, was my major source of income, or I should say, my only source of income. Dad or Aunt Mabel sent money when I had an urgent need for a particular item.

Smoking was allowed in the school but only in a designated area in the basement. Lockers for our nursing uniforms were located outside of the smoking room. We were required to take off the uniform and put on a robe. The breaks between classes were seven minutes, so several of us would make a mad dash out of the classroom, go to the basement, take off our uniforms and put on our robes, light up and take a few puffs, back to the locker, put on the uniform, run to class leaving the room blue with smoke and wondering if it was all worth it.

Our days included class time, floor time (a term used denoting time spent on a hospital unit), and practice time in the nursing arts room. Our first patients were one other: giving baths, injections, inserting nasal gastric tubes, and administering oxygen. In today's world, nursing schools have state-of-the-art mannequins that students practice on— but I think the benefit of hands on experience increased empathy for the patient.

Our first assignments were the passing of meal trays, offering bedpans and urinals, and helping with oral hygiene, a technical term for tooth brushing. About six weeks into our training we gave baths to patients. When giving a patient a bath it was with utmost respect, taking care not to expose the body any more than necessary.

The proper way to carry a meal tray was balancing it on your palm held above your shoulders. I am pretty confident that my right bicep was larger than the left after three years.

Bed-making was an art, with sheets drawn so tightly you could bounce a coin off them, and, of course, the corners of the linens had to be mitered perfectly.

All patient notes were hand-printed in their charts.

I believed in showing respect to doctors, but in 1955, showing respect was extreme—no matter how busy you were, you stood when a physician entered or acknowledged his presence by making eye contact or nodding your head.

Living together for three years helped develop a kinship between the students that would last a lifetime. I acquired three substitute mothers: Mrs. Willis, Mrs. Lipovitz, and Mrs. Wilson. They were the moms of fellow students Joan, Jane, and Mary. I particularly remember Mrs. Lipovitz for her kind ways and the cinnamon toast she'd make when I went with Jane to her home. Mrs. Wilson told me about hope chests and how girls my age filled them with embroidered pillowcases, doilies, and other items a new wife would need to start housekeeping. Mrs. Willis was a farm wife and a loving mother to her daughters. I loved it when Joan occasionally invited me to her home for the weekend. I maintained contact with these women throughout their lifetimes.

I wrote letters to Wayne on a weekly basis, usually the last thing before settling down for sleep. After Wayne's basic training in California, he was transferred to Eielson Air Force Base in Fairbanks, Alaska. His letters were descriptive about the weather conditions (once telling me the temperature plummeted to 55 below zero), animal life such as ptarmigans and bears, and having light for 21 hours in a day during the summer. The ptarmigan is an interesting bird from the grouse family. It has marble brown and reddish coloring with a black tail in the summer, but in the winter, turns white to blend in with the snowy background. It is the state bird of Alaska.

Of course, he wrote about missing me. In December of 1955, I not only received letters but a large package. I couldn't get to my room fast enough to open it. When I tore off the brown paper, I was faced with a pretty Christmas-wrapped gift and a sign, *DO NOT OPEN UNTIL CHRISTMAS*. It wasn't easy but I did it, in spite of a couple of my classmates urging me to open it. It was worth the wait—it was a hooded, rabbit fur Alaskan parka which I wore often—and appreciated during Wisconsin winters. My Aunt Mabel wasn't as excited. It was her feeling it wasn't appropriate for me to receive a personal gift when I was not engaged.

The Christmas of 1955 with my siblings was special. I stayed overnight at the Alland home (Mary's foster home) on December 23, and on the 24th my brother and sisters came to spend the day. It was wonderful with all of us in the same room and sitting down at the same table. My philosophy today is there is always room for one more and I truly believe I acquired that from Margaret Mary. She herself had four children, ages one to six, and yet found it in her heart to make Christmas special for the seven of us. I attended midnight mass with Mary and the Allands. The next day I visited Fred, Susan, and Patricia at the orphanage, and Barbara and Rita at their foster home. The remainder of the holiday season, Mary and I spent visiting Wayne's parents, my grampa, Aunt Isabel and Uncle Art, Dad and Aunt Mabel, and friends in Camp Douglas. Dad had dolls for me to give to the three littlest girls, which they loved very much.

*   *   *

1956

The New Year started with studying for final semester exams. We studied so hard we didn't allow time to go outside for a breath of fresh air. I hate to admit it but I did take time to go to the smoking room and have a cigarette. At the same time several students were battling colds or flu. It was only after receiving the test results that I could sigh a breath of relief.

We were called "probies" until the day designated as Capping Day, which was after six months of training. The cap signified we had passed the first hurdle. Dad, Grampa, and three of Mom's sisters attended: Isabel, Regina, and Clara. I know tears came to my eyes, wishing Mom were present.

As the months progressed, the intensity of our studies progressed as well. Having the support of fellow classmates was comforting and motivating when learning about the intricacies of our body systems, especially the skeletal, nervous, and muscular system which I found challenging to learn. I was aware of my body, but became even more aware when I learned I had 206 bones, approximately 650 muscles, and many, many nerves, but that wasn't all—we had to learn their names, location, and function. When one of us moaned and groaned and said, "I can't do this," there'd be someone who said with determination in her voice, *"Yes, you can."*

We rotated every three months to different units: surgical, medical, pediatrics, geriatrics, obstetrics, emergency room, operating room, dietary, and isolation. We were required to view an autopsy, and I was impressed how a pathologist showed dignity for the human body even while dissecting it.

As I rotated to the different units, I became aware of the type of nursing I wanted to practice, as well as what type of nursing I'd rather not practice, such as the operating room, the reason being the limited time the patient was awake. I preferred a conscious patient.

The operating room was exciting from the standpoint of seeing the inside of the body and actually seeing the location and look of body parts we learned about. Besides the surgeon, the team members included an anesthetist, scrub nurse, and a circulating nurse. The scrub nurse assisted the surgeon by holding retractors or handing instruments, and the circulating nurse worked outside the sterile field to be available to relay messages, take specimens to the lab, do sponge count, or procure needed supplies. One of the first specimens I had to deliver to the lab as a circulating nurse was an amputated leg. As I walked down the hall to the lab I prayed the leg would not fall out of the specimen pan.

*   *   *

Wayne came home on leave in June of 1956. I was very happy he made it because there was a question about him getting his furlough. Wayne worked as a propeller mechanic on the airbase and B-29s were being replaced by B-50s, so it was necessary for the mechanics to learn the intricacies of the new planes, but it all worked out. I took my two-week vacation and we didn't waste a minute of it.

Wayne used his family's vehicle to come to La Crosse to pick me up. It was good to see him, and hug him, and kiss him. Nine months had passed but the tingles were still there. I knew his time home would pass by quickly. I asked if we could visit all the kids before heading to New Lisbon and Lyndon Station. He didn't say, 'no' but I sensed he wasn't overly enthused. *One thing I'm certain of is, any mate of mine will need to have a vested interest in helping me not lose track of my family.*

Wayne and I were able to stay at Mr. and Mrs. Senn's (foster parents of Rita and Barbara) home one night, giving us the time to see everybody. Wayne bunked out in the living room in a sleeping bag, which he didn't seem to mind. After leaving the Senn home, we visited Dad, as Wayne hadn't met him. Dad asked questions about his work in the Air Force and what his plans would be after the service. *Dad is already worrying about my future. I suppose that is good.* Aunt Mabel took me aside during Dad and Wayne's conversation reminding me I was in nursing school and not to rush into anything. *I think I have already rushed into something. I love him and often imagine a future together.* "Thanks, Aunt Mabel. I'll try."

After leaving La Crosse we stayed at Wayne's home in Lyndon Station for a few days. I always enjoyed visits to his home. His parents, Gladys and Earl, were so welcoming and his sister, Rosalie, was happy to have someone besides brothers to be with. One of my first visits was to Christy's Café to see Christy, Warren, and Paulette. Of course, they wanted to know how nurse's training was going, as well as how my brother and sisters were doing.

We made a trip to South Bend, Indiana to visit Wayne's aunt and uncle. They had several children, close in age, but children definitely born to the right parents. As I watched parents and offspring interacting, I could feel their love. I remember making a comment to Wayne, *my* wish to have a big family, and being tearfully devastated when he remarked that he didn't know if he wanted children or not. *Having children is in my destiny, God willing.*

We returned to Lyndon Station after a few days. A couple of days before our vacation was coming to an end, Wayne and I'd been out for the evening. As I was sliding across the seat to get out of the car, he touched my arm and said, "Don't go in just yet. I have something to ask you." He reached across me and opened the glove compartment, taking out a small box which he handed to me. My hands shook as I opened it. When I saw the diamond ring, my heart was racing in high gear and I probably was blushing; I blushed easily. Wayne took the ring, and reaching for my hand, said, "I love you, Rose, and hope you will accept this engagement ring." During the seconds that followed I was excited and yet apprehensive. I couldn't forget what he said about not wanting children, but I loved him, and said yes. As we embraced, I hoped I was making the right decision.

We went into the house and shared the news. His sister, Rosalie, seemed the most excited, "I'm going to have a sister!" When I looked at the faces of Wayne's mom, dad, and brothers, I knew this family had accepted me. Of course, his brothers, Carl and Bud, had to do a little teasing, "You know you two can't look at another gal or guy now."

The remaining days of our vacation went by quickly, especially knowing we wouldn't see one another until August of 1957. Wayne returned to the airbase in Alaska, and I to the nurse's dorm. News traveled fast that I was engaged.

Everyone wanted to see my ring, and I proudly extended my hand to show it off.

As the months went by, I began to feel more and more like a nurse and realized I liked that feeling. It wasn't always pleasant, especially when I experienced the death of one of my patients who died of a myocardial infarction; in layman's terms, a massive heart attack. We were told to hold our emotions inside, but I couldn't. After the physician pronounced him dead, and I had to prepare the body, which meant closing the eyelids if necessary, cleansing the body if needed, and covering with a sheet, the tears streamed down my cheeks. The family noticed my tears, and I was OK with that—they knew I cared.

I will never forget little Julie, diagnosed with spinal meningitis. Her hospital crib seemed to devour her. She looked so vulnerable, but never complained, and always had a smile, even if it took all the energy she could muster. I knew someday if I had a girl I would name her Julie.

And then there was my patient with mouth cancer. The odor from his cancer was so horrific that we put towels in the space under the door to keep the smell from seeping into the hallway and into other rooms. When I was assigned to him I used to think leper colonies would have been comparable. Here was another patient who didn't complain, but I think secretly he wished the Lord would take him. He was embarrassed that we had to do his mouth care and endure the odor. *Whatsoever you do to the least of my brethren so you shall do unto me.*

I continued to visit my sibs on a regular basis. Mary Ann, Barbara, and Rita seemed to adjust well to their foster homes. I was sad that homes hadn't been found for Patricia, Susan, and Fred.

My dad worked in the La Crosse area for about a year and rented a room at the Milner Hotel, which gave me the opportunity to meet him for lunch on occasion. He surprised me at one of those lunches by giving me a rhinestone necklace, which was in style at that time. I still have it.

1957

Toward the end of 1956 I had increased pain with menstruation, necessitating a doctor's appointment. On examination, the physician felt a mass in my lower abdomen. I was scheduled for exploratory surgery in January 1957 for a suspected tumor.

"Rose, can you hear me?" It was Dr. Pauley. "You had a tumor and we had to remove your left ovary and fallopian tube. You may not be able to conceive."

Doesn't he know I'd like a dozen children? Mom, I wish you were here. I'd love to feel the comfort of your hand, your hand that held mine so firmly on my first day of school when I was crossing a busy street.

After five days in the hospital, I recovered at the foster home of my sisters, Barbara and Rita, for one month. Mrs. Senn took good care of me, and a plus was seeing my sisters at the end of their school day and on the weekends. Mr. and Mrs. Senn had two daughters of their own, Lenore and Cathy, so between the four girls I received lots of attention, and was given many handmade cards and drawings. Mr. Senn made regular trips to the nursing school to pick up assignments for me to work on.

I had my first assignment to write an article for the St. Francis School of Nursing paper. Mrs. Mairich, the school secretary, thought it'd be beneficial for me to write my experience of being a patient. In our nursing arts class, we learned the phrase "roll the patient like a log" in one smooth movement, especially if the patient had abdominal surgery, to eliminate additional discomfort. Most of the time during my hospital stay I was rolled to my side the correct way, but having someone move me in a jerky fashion was a lesson learned. It made me feel like my insides were being torn apart, and I never wanted a patient I cared for to experience that. Likewise wetting a patient's lips with water when he or she is unable to have food and drink, is a gift. It seems like such a simple thing to do, but so well received. I was grateful for the experience of being a patient.

* * *

Knowledge of psychiatry was part of our nursing requirements. St. Francis Hospital didn't have a psychiatric unit, which necessitated going to Mendota State Hospital in Madison, for our psychiatric affiliation. I was assigned to go in June, July, and August of 1957. I was excited for several reasons. I was looking forward to seeing the city of Madison, the capital; I was anticipating being in new surroundings and had a feeling I would like psychiatry, which I did.

We had to arrange our own transportation from La Crosse to Madison, most likely I rode with another student's family. Mendota State Hospital was situated on several acres bordering Lake Mendota on the northeast side of the city. It was a sprawling complex of new and old structures. Upon entering the grounds I noticed an antiquated multistory building, whose appearance gave me an eerie feeling. I'd learn the patients' quarters in this building were referred to as: Old Female 4 and Old Male 6. They housed the severely mentally ill residents.

Student housing was a two-story building with private quarters and a live-in housemother, Mrs. Newman.

The newer structures included Lorenz Hall, an admission and treatment unit for men and women, a centrally located cafeteria for the staff, and Goodland Hall, also for residents.

The back of the property was wooded, with mostly tall, thin pine trees, interspersed with one-story buildings connected by sidewalks. Some of these buildings were employee housing. Dr. Urban, the administrator, had a regular home on the property with a view of Lake Mendota. Today the home, which was built in 1932, is a historical landmark.

A building I'd become familiar with was the recreational center, where patients would be escorted for occupational therapy. It was there I learned to play billiards and cribbage, as well as how to weave.

My vocabulary expanded with terms like hallucinations, schizophrenia, catatonia, manic depressive disorder, and other psychiatric terminology.

A set of keys became an appendage, as every door required a key for entry and exit. We were instructed to protect the keys with our lives to prevent a patient from stealing them.

The knowledge I gained from the psychiatric experience helped me many times in my journey of life. It helped me be a better listener, to be empathetic, and maybe in ways helped me to be nonjudgmental in regard to my mom.

*   *   *

One day in the dorm, a fellow student hollered down the hall that some guy she knew was there and would take as many girls as would fit in the car to a nearby root beer stand.

There must have been six or seven of us crammed in the car, some of us double-decker; no seat belts back then. Don was the driver and he had a friend named Mike with him. I was in the back seat at the bottom of the pile. We arrived at the root beer stand, piled out, ordered our drinks and burgers, chatted back and forth, piled back into the car, and returned to the dorm.

About two hours later, Mrs. Newman, the housemother, could be heard in the hall, "Rose Steinmetz, you have a telephone call."

"A telephone call?" I asked myself. "I don't know anyone in Madison."

I marched down to the end of the hall and took the receiver from Mrs. Newman.

"Hello?" I said in a questioning voice.

"Hi, this is Mike."

"Mike who?"

"Mike Bingham. You caught my eye when we went to the root beer stand."

"I don't know how you ever noticed me. I was buried in that car."

"Well, I did notice you and I'd like to see you again."

"I'm engaged. I'll only see you if a bunch of us nurses are out as a group."

"Fair enough. I hope that happens soon."

I hung up the phone in disbelief, thinking I probably wouldn't recognize him if I saw him. *I still can't believe he noticed me.*

I did see Mike again on several occasions, but with others present. There were trips to Vilas Zoo, or the outdoor theater, or just hanging out. Mike had a way of singling me out and in a teasing way asking if I was still engaged, even when he knew what the answer would be. There was something very likable about him. He had a great sense of humor and a gift of gab, but under that, I sensed he was caring, honest, and sincere. I liked him. *Rose, you haven't seen Wayne for a year. Don't become infatuated with Mike. Wayne will be home soon, and you'll realize he is still the one.* On one of those outings, Mike took me aside and asked if I would go on a date with him, by myself. I hesitated, and then looked right at him and said, "It's a deal, but I'm still engaged." *My heart is beating so hard. I should just tell him no.*

It was easier agreeing to go out with Mike, because of a recent letter I had received from Wayne. I hadn't seen my sibs for two months, so I wrote Wayne asking if he'd drive me to La Crosse to see them when he came home in August. I was saddened when his response shouted it was *me* he wanted to see, and not my brother and sisters. I realized he hadn't seen me for over a year, but…

On our date I learned Mike had been discharged from the army in February. He took his basic training, and attended cook's school at Fort Leonard Wood, Missouri. After eighteen months he was sent overseas to Korea where he cooked for the officers. He shared with me gut-wrenching details of Korean mothers and their children, peering through the fences, with looks of despair, as they watched the cooks dispose of food as they broke up camp. The cooks, knowing they could be court-martialed, dug shallow trenches along the fence line, put food in protective covering, and left it to be dug up after they left. I knew Mike had a generous heart when he related his experience.

I learned he was born in Madison, the youngest of nine children, and had been poor growing up. His dad was 59 and mother 39 when he was born. He talked respectfully about his parents and siblings. He lived with his parents. He worked two jobs, one at a service station, and the other at a Caramel Crisp shop, but hoped for something better.

I felt comfortable sharing the story of my mom's disappearance, and about my siblings being in foster homes, and of the three still in the orphanage, and most of all how important it was that I stayed involved with them and not lose contact. I couldn't believe it when he said, "If you need to go and see them before your affiliation is completed, I'd be happy to drive you."

The hours passed by more quickly than I would have liked, but curfew was 10 p.m. When Mike's car stopped in front of the dorm, I thanked him for a great time. All we did was talk, but it was so easy talking with one another. He leaned toward me. I knew he wanted to kiss me and I wanted him to, but I put up my hand, palm facing toward him, and said, "I really need to wait until Wayne comes home, so I can sort out my feelings."

"So there is hope."

"Just wait."

*   *   *

I was nervous the day I knew Wayne would be coming to see me. I was up in my dorm room packing clothes for the weekend. We were going to his parents' home in Lyndon Station, and to La Crosse to see my brother and sisters. Wayne agreed to this after I replied to his letter telling him how important it was to me.

There was a knock on my door. It was Mrs. Newman, the housemother. "Miss Steinmetz, there is someone to see you."

I grabbed my purse and weekend bag and proceeded to the first floor. Wayne was standing in the entryway looking as handsome as when he left, maybe more mature. He was blessed with a beautiful head of hair, striking eyes, and an infectious smile. What was there not to love? I embraced him, "Welcome home. A year is a long time."

He stepped back, placed his hands on my shoulders and said," Let me get a good look at you, Squirt. You've changed but in a good way."

"So have you. I see you're sporting a mustache. I like it."

"Well, let's get going. Mom is eager to see you. She says she hasn't seen you since Christmas."

"I know. When I do have time off, it is valuable time to study. It will be good to see her today."

Wayne took my suitcase from me as I was signing out for the weekend. "I'm signed out, Mrs. Newman. I'll be back on Sunday."

We walked out to the parking area. Although it was only midmorning, I knew it was going to be a hot, humid August day.

Wayne opened the car door for me, and placed my suitcase in the back seat. As he was walking around the car to get in, I took a deep breath in anticipation of approaching the subject of Mike. It wasn't like I was dating him or anything, but I had doubts about my feelings for him *and* Wayne. Someone was going to be hurt based on my decision, and I didn't want that. Wayne settled himself behind the steering wheel. The car windows were open allowing some air movement.

Maybe Wayne thinks I'm not cuddling close to him because of the warm temperature, when in fact I don't want to sit close because I don't want him to think everything's OK.

"Wayne—," I started to say, when Wayne said, "Rose, we need to talk."

"I need to talk, too. There's this guy, Mike, but it's not what you might think. A bunch of us from the dorm have gone on outings. One of the nurses has a friend, Don, and Don has a friend, Mike, who comes with him. I'm not sure what it is about Mike, but I feel I'd like to get to know him better. I'm so confused. I'm hoping being with you for the weekend will answer some questions for me."

"Rose, it's OK. What *I* wanted to talk about is we giving each other permission to date. I love you, but think about it—our actual time together has been about six weeks. Are we ready to make a lifelong commitment?"

I sure didn't expect this. I wonder if this came about because of my commitment to my brother and sisters, or our conversation last summer about having children?

We drove in silence for several miles. I wished I'd waited to bring this all up when we were out of the car and could make eye contact. It was hard talking to each other, when he had to keep his eyes on the road. *What* Wayne said made sense, and it was what I wanted, too. My thoughts shifted to Gladys, Wayne's mother, and the disappointment she would feel. She had told me more than once she was happy I was going to be her daughter-in-law.

"Wayne, how are we going to tell your mother if we decide to end our relationship?"

"Rose, you don't have to end *your* relationship with my mom. I know how much she has meant to you, especially with the loss—"

"Wayne, please don't say *loss*. My mom disappeared and maybe someday she may be back. *Loss* sounds so final."

"I'm sorry." He removed his right hand from the steering wheel and squeezed my hand.

"I hope we can still go to La Crosse tomorrow and see my family. I told them we'd be coming for the day."

He glanced at me and said," Yes, we'll go to La Crosse. I know how much it means to you."

"Thanks, Wayne. A really big thanks."

As we continued driving to Lyndon Station, I was aware I was twisting my engagement ring back and forth on my finger, knowing it wouldn't be there by the end of the weekend. Would Mike notice when I returned to Madison?

We talked to Wayne's parents shortly after we arrived at the house. It wasn't an easy conversation but they understood. When I expressed my wish to Gladys to maintain contact with her, she embraced me, and whispered in my ear, "You'll always be my daughter."

I whispered back, "And you, my other mother."

The visit to La Crosse to see my siblings brought cheerfulness to the weekend. It appeared they had all shot up an inch or two over the summer. They were looking forward to the new school year. It was good to be able to tell them I would be back in La Crosse at the end of August.

Sister Bertina at the orphanage informed me Social Services staff was actively seeking foster homes for Fred, Susan, and Patricia.

Wayne drove me back to Madison. Most of our conversation during the drive was wishing each other happiness. When he stopped the car at the dorm, I leaned over and kissed him on the cheek and handed him the ring. *I've heard each relationship prepares you for the relationship that is meant to be. I hope that is true.* I saw Wayne on one occasion after that day. It was at his dad's funeral in 1960.

At times, I would lie in bed trying to make sense of all that happened. I never stopped loving Wayne; I just met someone I loved more.

I finished my psychiatric affiliation at the end of August. It was difficult leaving Madison because it was difficult leaving Mike. In the short time we had, about two weeks, we saw each other as much as possible. I met his folks, who were dear, down-to-earth people who made me feel very welcome in their presence.

September of 1957 was the start of my third year of nurse's training. That last year seemed to be an acceleration of responsibility, expectations, and time spent on the units. We were able to pick a specialty for advanced nursing skills. I chose the pediatric unit where I was able to spend six weeks working more closely with the head nurse. One of the procedures I did, under the supervision of a physician, was to start an intravenous drip on an infant using a vein on the scalp. I still can visualize that tiny head, and the needle that seemed so large, and hoping what I was doing was not too painful for the baby.

We were also required to do case studies, which were an excellent learning tool. A case study required the medical history, diagnosis, symptoms, medication and treatment plan, prognosis, and patient's outcome. Even today I can remember three of my case studies: myocardial infarction, cirrhosis of the liver, and spinal meningitis. All case studies were due on July 17, 1958.

During my last year in La Crosse, Mike visited me whenever he could, and I made visits to Madison when I had a weekend off. On a weekend in July of 1958, I took a Greyhound bus to Madison to see him. Mike, his friend, Denis, and I went to Conklin Beach, a beach a few blocks from Mike's home. I liked Denis. Mike had shared with me they had been friends since childhood. Denis was an only child, so Mike was like a brother. Mike told me, as a kid, he enjoyed going to Denis' house, especially for breakfast, when he could have as many eggs as he was able to eat. Mike's family had to portion food out so there was enough for everyone.

The beach area was full of squealing children eager to go into the water, and cautious parents instructing them to be patient. We found a spot among other sun worshipers, and stretched out our blanket. I had my suit on under my clothing and felt self-conscious as I took off my pedal-pushers and blouse; Mike had never seen me in a swimming suit. *I hope my legs are clean-shaven. I forgot to check.* I put on my swimming cap and tucked in loose strands of hair. As I tip-toed into the water and was enjoying the feeling of sand between my toes, Mike and Denis entered like torpedoes ejected from a warship, and were nowhere to be seen, until I felt myself being lifted by Mike out of the water.

"Please, don't dunk me!"

He didn't. He gently turned me so I was facing him, and planted a sweet, wet kiss on my lips. I told him how special it was swimming in Lake Mendota, compared to a creek or river. The special feeling was interrupted as we found ourselves in the crossfire of splashing water warfare. We returned to the beach blanket. While Mike and I chatted, Denis was busy reading a book. I was distracted wondering how my hair looked since I took off the swimming cap, and was trying to finger-comb it, when I heard Mike say, "You look fine. I'd like to marry you."

I looked at him and then at Denis and back at him, "You're not kidding, are you?"

"No, I'm not. Denis is my witness."

I remember telling him, without the benefit of moonlight, and in the presence of his best friend, Denis, that it must be real, and I accepted.

During the last half of the year I started sending out applications for available positions. My applications were sent to St. Mary's Hospital and the Children's Diagnostic Center in Madison. I was accepted at St. Mary's and started employment there on September 5, 1958.

1958 was a good year for my brother and sisters at the orphanage. Little Patricia went to the foster home of Jack and Margaret Marcou in February. The Marcous had three children of their own: Judy, John, and Michael.

Fred went for temporary placement to my Aunt Isabel and Uncle Art's farm in June, and later that year to the home of Joe and Coletta Stevens, who lived on a farm in Cashton, which was about a half hour drive from La Crosse. Joe and Coletta had no children of their own but over the years had several foster sons.

There was correspondence from a social worker to my dad informing him that I would be accompanying her to visit a prospective foster home for my brother. In the letter, she wrote: "I will know if the home meets Rose's approval by the look on her face."

On December 19, Susan went to the home of Frank and Dorothy Zahn, who had no children. This was such a relief for me, knowing I'd be leaving the La Crosse area after graduation, and visits to see my family would be limited because of distance and new job responsibilities.

Although we were at the nursing school until August, our graduation ceremony was May 25, 1958. I had to pinch myself realizing my dreams had come true. I was close to being a registered nurse. Grampa Debovik, Aunt Regina and Aunt Clara (Mom's sisters), Uncle Frank, and Uncle John came from Illinois. I felt special thinking they had driven all that way to help me celebrate my accomplishment.

Dad didn't attend my graduation ceremonies. I don't recall when I learned the reason my dad wasn't there was because he was in Waupun State Prison for non-support of our care at St. Michael's Orphanage. My Aunt Mabel told me. He was imprisoned from February 15, 1958, to April

21, 1959. I wrote frequently to him at the Waupun address: Box C, Waupun, Wisconsin, not knowing it was the Wisconsin State Prison. I thought he had a painting contract. It saddened me when I found out, because I know from correspondence from my dad he was not lax in looking for work.

Over the post-graduate years, my nursing passion would come to be in the areas of pediatrics, medical conditions, post-surgical care, developmental disabilities, and psychiatric nursing. After graduating in 1958, my first job was one year on a medical/surgical unit at St. Mary's Hospital in Madison. I then worked at Mendota State Hospital for three years for reasons of better pay. I chose not to be employed during the years 1960-1964 because of having babies.

In 1964, I went to work at Central Wisconsin Center for the Developmentally Disabled and left in 1988 when we relocated to Lodi, Wisconsin. I worked at Sauk Prairie Memorial Hospital primarily as a nurse manager on a medical/surgical unit until my retirement in 2001. The nursing profession was challenging, rewarding, and a job where I often went home tired, but not tired of going back the next day.

Chapter 19
A New Life as
Mrs. Michael Bingham

I left my "home" of three years with mixed emotions. I was happy I had completed nursing school, but sad saying good bye to fellow nurses, who had become like sisters. I felt nervous anticipation about moving to a more populated city, Madison, Wisconsin. The hardest part was assuring my brother and sisters I wouldn't lose contact with them. *Like a dominant-colored thread in a tapestry, my thoughts of Mom and keeping contact with my family were woven into my life.*

Mike had come to the dorm and helped me load up my belongings. He rented a U-Haul because I had a cedar chest (a graduation gift from Barbara and Rita's foster parents, Mr. and Mrs. Senn), as well as all my possessions. Before getting into his car, I recall looking up at the school and doing a fast rewind of three years of memories: nights of cramming for exams, tears, laughter, and a special sister-hood with my classmates.

I moved into a quaint brick house one block off State Street, a street that ran from the Capital Square to the University campus area. I shared the house with three young women who had secretarial jobs. I remember their perplexed faces as they looked at all Mike and I hauled into the house. I guess one could have compared me to a hermit crab: carrying my house with me wherever I went. I decided to explain my situation to them right on the spot. They listened attentively and verbalized compassion, but more than that, a realized that maybe they should be a bit more appreciative of their mothers.

We found places for all my belongings, with items I wouldn't be using going under the bed.

Mike and I told them we'd be married at the end of November, and therefore I'd be renting for only three months. I was pleased the landlord permitted a month-to-month lease.

Mike gave me a big hug and a smooch and told me he'd see me the next day. I thanked him much, walked him to the door, and waited until he drove away. I took a deep breath and went inside.

The first order of business was discussing household re-sponsibilities. Sarah made her wishes known immediately. She verbalized she'd prefer cleaning or laundry, anything but cooking. I told her I hadn't done any cooking for four years, so we might work together and learn as we went. Bonnie seemed to be a happy spirit, saying, "I'll do what-ever. Just give me a job." Jane's business-like personality became apparent when she announced she'd take responsi-bility for making out a list, with the various chores rotated week to week. I told Jane and the others that I would need some flexibility, as my hours wouldn't be 9-to-5 working at St. Mary's Hospital.

My first impressions of my new friends were positive.

I ended up living there one month.

It was a weekday and my day off. My roommates were at work, and I was studying for my state board exams. Occasional horn honking interrupted the quietness in the house. I was stretched out on my bed reading the *Mosby*

Comprehensive Review for Nursing State Board Exams. A wave of dizziness came over me as I was getting up to get a glass of water. I sat down on the edge of the bed and thought to myself, what was that all about? *No, don't even think that. Periods can be late and, besides, Dr. Pauly said I would have difficulty conceiving as a result of my surgery for an ovarian tumor. But, Mike and I did make love. I remember the date. It was his dad's 82nd birthday and such a celebration it was. I guess we carried the celebration well into the night.*

I shared my suspicions with Mike that evening. He didn't say, "Are you sure?" He lovingly took me in his arms and said everything would be OK.

A pregnancy urine test confirmed my suspicions. Mike's reaction was positive, but inside I was happy we were already engaged. I wouldn't have wanted him to marry me just because I was carrying his child.

On September 27, Mike and I went to the City County building and filled out marriage license forms. The plan was for Mike to pick me up on the morning of the 28th after the girls left for work and travel to Dubuque, Iowa, to be married by the Justice of the Peace. I loved Mike and knew he would take good care of me, but I was nervous and feeling guilty I wasn't being married in the Catholic church. We were eloping, so Dad and Mike's parents wouldn't know until after the fact. Actually, Mike's mom knew but we didn't know she knew. I'm sure she thought Mike was joking when she asked what his plans were for the day and he replied, as he was going out the door, "It is Rose's day off. We're going to get married."

September 28 was a beautiful day with clear blue skies, an abundance of sunshine and brilliant fall color. I cuddled up close to Mike, no seat belts back then, and thought to myself, in a couple of hours, I'll be Mrs. Michael Bingham.

That night I remember standing in the bathroom of the motel in my beautiful negligee, Mike waiting for me in bed, and I being so nervous. Obviously we'd made love before, but saying, "I do" was a lifetime commitment. *Dear God, help me be a good wife and mother.* I walked out into the bedroom.

*   *   *

We lived with Mike's folks for one month and then moved into a four-unit apartment on Brooks Street, one block from the hospital. We were on the second level. We furnished our entire apartment for $500. A furniture store in Madison offered a package deal that included: double bed and dresser, a chrome dining room set with four chairs, a blue couch, two end tables, and two lamps. We paid for the furniture, and in anticipation of our little one, we put a $20 crib on lay-away and paid five dollars a month.

The first night in our apartment probably caused wonderment by the downstairs tenant. Mike and I had crawled into our newly set-up bed, only to have the mattress and springs crash to the floor. The bed slats had been the wrong size.

The neighbors I remember were Mr. and Mrs. Fisher who owned the apartment and lived across the street, Al and Betty Pedracine, owners of a local business, who lived in one of the downstairs units, and a military officer and his wife who lived across the hall from us. Mr. Fisher was a caring landlord who told us about the importance of rental insurance, and about basic tools one should have, namely, a hammer, pliers, screwdriver, yardstick, and a few nails.

Living one block from the hospital was convenient, as I didn't drive. My job was as a staff nurse on a medical/surgical unit. I wanted to work in pediatrics, but there were no open positions. I enjoyed my job and worked with fine physicians and nursing staff. Those first few months I whispered frequently to myself, "Pinch me, and tell me I'm not dreaming. **I am a registered nurse."**

My sister, Mary, entered St. Mary's School of Nursing in September of 1958. It was comforting to have one of my family members so close. She often would stay overnight when she had a weekend off. The nurses' dorm was adjacent to the hospital so she was able to walk to our apartment. Her visits were especially nice since my doctor instructed me not to make visits to La Crosse to see my sibs in the last two months of my pregnancy.

In December 1958, Mike agreed to profess our marriage vows at St. James Catholic Church. Mike didn't become Catholic, but agreed to raise our children as Catholics. He attended marriage preparation classes but was unable to accept the sacrament of Penance. We had a small ceremony in the rectory, with my sister, Mary, and Mike's best friend, Denis, as witnesses. Mike's family had a reception for us. I remember sitting on the floor of our living room later in the day, touching, holding, and appreciating the gifts we had received. Not all the gifts were household items. Mike's childhood friends, Lucy, Karen, and Becky, had given me the most beautiful satin, lace-trimmed slip. When I wore that slip, I wished it were *over* my dress so everyone could see it, but *I* knew it was there. I could feel the satin brush against my legs as I walked. When my tummy started to expand, I reluctantly tucked the slip away in a drawer.

I remember the day I wore a maternity smock for the first time. It was my day off and Mike was at work at John Deere Implement. I was standing at the stove when Mike came home from work. I felt beautiful, and looked forward to wearing maternity clothes out in public. People would know I was with child. I hoped Mike would think I was beautiful as well. With my back to Mike, I said, "Hi, honey. Did you have a good day?" I turned around. He noticed. He walked over, hugged me, and patted my abdomen, saying, "You look radiant." I hugged him back.

"How could I not look radiant? It's a miracle I'm even pregnant."

*   *   *

I have regrets about our first Christmas. Mike came home with a "Charlie Brown" tree, which in hindsight I should have been happy about.

"How much did you pay for that tree?"

"Ten dollars."

"It hardly has any branches."

He liked the tree, but took it out of our apartment and purchased a different one. Flocking of Christmas trees was popular in 1958, so we flocked it white. I started getting nauseated before we could get the ornaments on. You guessed it—he had to purchase tree number three. The tree was adorned with a total of fourteen ornaments, and icicles draped over the branches. Today, I have many more ornaments, but those fourteen are the first to go on the tree each year. Ten of those ornaments were purchased from Woolworth's Five and Dime, for a grand total of three dollars.

Our baby's due date was May 5, 1959, but he opted to arrive on April 21, nine days before my health insurance went into effect.

I thought of my mom during those five days in the hospital, wishing I could have told her all about her first grandchild. I had observed the birth of several babies during my obstetric rotation in nursing school, and each birth was a miracle that brought me to tears. I often wondered if that awesome feeling ever dimmed. When I gave birth to our son, words were not adequate to describe the ultimate joy I experienced. I would have asked Mom if she felt similar joy with each of her seven babies.

We named him Michael Carl, Michael, after his dad and grandpa, and Carl, after Mike's brother-in-law. Giving him the middle name of Carl must have been a premonition as Betty and Carl would be two of the first people to get acquainted with little Michael. I was discharged from the hospital on April 26. On the morning of the 27th, Mike came into the bedroom and said he was ready to leave for his job at John Deere Implement Company. He kissed me and then went over to the bassinet and kissed little Michael on the top of his head.

Being awakened, I got up to use the bathroom. As I sat on the toilet, I felt intense pressure in my vaginal area, almost like when I gave birth. I sensed a feeling of doom, and screamed as loud as I could, hoping Mike would hear me before he got in his car. I passed an enormous clot and knew I was hemorrhaging. Everything went black.

*   *   *

I heard a loud voice, "Hurry, we need a type and cross match. We're losing her." I opened my eyes. I couldn't focus…I remembered. I tried to scream. I heard no sound. Questions were floating in my head. "My baby, I need to take care of my baby."

I heard a familiar voice. It was Mike's. "Honey, you are in the hospital."

"Where is little Michael?"

"He's OK, honey. He's with our neighbor."

I realized about seven that evening just how serious my medical condition had been when a man looked into my room, stared at my face and uttered, "Oh, the woman who was in this room earlier must have died."

I answered back, "I've been in this room since early morning."

If Mike had not heard my screams, I would not be writing this story. I was hemorrhaging and would have died within a couple of hours.

Chapter 20
The Sixties

We moved from our first apartment a couple of months after Michael was born into another apartment near Mendota State Hospital, where I took a job following my three-month maternity leave. It meant a $100 increase in wages; I was close enough to walk to work, and little Michael had an exceptional babysitter named Mrs. Tunberg.

Mike left John Deere Implement Company when he qualified for a radial drill operator apprenticeship at Gisholt Machine Company on East Washington Avenue in Madison. As a couple we were excited, as it paid a decent salary and it was a job with room for growth. The Gisholt plant closed, unfortunately, not long after we purchased our first home. Mike took a job with Omar Bakeries, which delivered bread and pastries door to door. The area he covered was a rural route outside of Madison. The money was good but I saw little of him because of the long hours.

We purchased our first home in 1960 for $16,800. It was in a new residential development on the northeast side of Madison, on land that had been a pig farm. Neither Mike's nor my parents had ever bought a home so it was special for us. It was possible because we were able to get a veteran's loan with no down payment.

The day of our closing we were handed the house keys, which I rubbed gently between my fingers, anticipating walking to the front door and putting it into the keyhole.

When we opened the door the smell of fresh paint and new lumber welcomed us. My footsteps echoed as I walked from room to room, decorating ideas racing through my head. *Maybe Patricia would be able to stay for a weekend, or Mary or Freddy or Susan or Barbara and Rita. I have room.* My thoughts were interrupted by friends saying, "Rose and Mike, tell us where you'd like us to put things."

A bird's eye view of the development was one of three-bedroom, single-story homes looking as if they were dropped into a field void of trees. We found out in a hurry what it meant to be a homeowner: growing a lawn from scratch, removing stones and rocks, spreading wheelbarrow loads of black dirt, scattering seed and straw, watering, but being very excited when you peeked under the straw and saw those beautiful green sprouts appearing.

With a one year old, and expecting a second child in October of 1960 (Michelle Rene), we had a fence put around the backyard. I looked forward to the first spring I could plant a garden. I had a three by two-foot area at the last apartment where I planted petunias, so I became giddy thinking about a large garden filled with an assortment of vegetables and bordered by zinnias, much like Dad's garden. I purchased a book about plotting out the vegetable garden and at night when Michael and Michelle were asleep, I sketched out my garden plan. McKay Nursery helped us with an affordable selection of foundation plants and trees.

The rooms were not carpeted in our new home. We had area rugs in the bedrooms and planned on wall-to-wall carpeting in the living room. Our third child, Julie, was born December 19, 1961, so budgeting was a necessity.

Mike applied at the post office and the Madison Fire Department, and there was a chance Gisholt would reopen. Wouldn't you know it? —Mike received acceptance letters from all three places. I remember the two of us up until the wee hours of the morning wrestling with all the options: Gisholt might close again, the post office job was the night shift, and the fire department had 24-hour shifts. Mike decided it would be difficult to sleep during the day with three little children up and about, so accepted the position as a fireman in February 1962. He was on the department for 27 years, and the job served our family well.

It wasn't until the spring of 1962 that we felt we could afford carpeting and were excited as we pondered over color, design, and durability features. We listened to the salesperson tell us Mohawk carpeting was of good quality and yet within our price range. We learned good padding made not so expensive carpeting feel *plush*. I was looking forward to walking on plush.

Everything was done except picking out the installment date for laying the carpet. Mike came home from a shift at the firehouse excited about a used police boat for sale at Tofte's Marina. "One of the guys at the station said it's a motorboat and in good shape. I could go fishing on Lake Mendota and we could go on boat rides. The kids would love it."

"The kids? They are three and under. How would they know?"

Mike's face shone like sunshine, but I felt like a black cloud just came over us. "Honey, I don't think we can afford new carpeting *and* a boat."

The disappointed look on his face was like watching an eclipse of the sun. I knew what I had to do. "Honey, go check out the boat. If you buy it, we will name it *Mohawk*."

It was the beginning of April 1963. While doing dishes I was looking out the window above the sink surveying the backyard, almost not believing even after two and a half

years it was *our* backyard. On the left side was my clothesline, diapers flapping in the wind. Across the backyard was
my garden waiting for spring planting, which was going
to be a challenge with my expanding tummy in the way.
I would be giving birth to our fourth child in June. To the
right of the garden were the swing set and the sand box
waiting to be climbed on by the little ones. That day they
were playing in the toy area in the basement.

As I continued doing the dishes I thought I smelled
smoke. I turned to see if a cigarette was smoldering in
the ashtray on the cupboard and was startled by one of
the kids shouting, "Mommy!" I opened the door leading to the basement. I could barely see the kids through
the smoke. Somehow, I got all three of them up the stairs,
stopping at the phone in the kitchen to call the fire department, and grabbing coats. Besides our safety, I was
thinking of Mike hearing over the loudspeaker in the
fire station: "Fire at 1514 Arizona Pass." When the fire
truck pulled up, I shouted, "We are all OK. The fire is in
the basement."

*Please God, I pray the fire can be contained in the basement
area. My personal life is in that house—photos of Mom, Dad, my
brother and sisters, diplomas and mementos.* I looked down at
the kids huddled close to me and realized they were what
mattered the most, and we were safe. A smile came to my
face when I noticed I had put one of my coats on Michelle's
little two-and-a-half-year-old body. Only her little face was
visible. It was as though the coat swallowed her.

The fire was contained to the basement but the smoke
damage was unbelievable. It found its way into every corner of the house, including the insides of dresser drawers.
When I was able to go into the house I was not prepared for
the after-effects of the fire. The odor of smoke hung heavy

in the air. Wisps of soot had settled on the floors, furniture, and drapery. I had a clothesline in the basement lined with charred clothespins. The children's toys had been transfigured into unidentifiable globs of plastic, metal frames of toy trucks with no rubber wheels, and charred pull toys with no strings. Fire inspectors first thought one of our children might have started the fire but Mike and I were diligent about keeping matches out of reach. After further investigation, the inspectors concluded the fire started as a result of a leak in the gas meter.

Laura and Clem, neighbors who lived one house down from us, invited us to their home, not just for the day, but for a week or more while our house was made livable again. They had five children of their own but assured us it would work and it did. They were Julie's godparents and enjoyed the time with her.

Being inexperienced, Mike and I didn't realize our insurance company could have authorized temporary living quarters, but since we didn't ask, they didn't offer. I swear the man they sent to clean up the house and paint had never done anything similar before, or if he had, workmanship was not a priority. He was at our house for about an hour and I said to Mike, "I know we can do this better."

It was a miracle our little Mary was born without incident after the eight weeks I spent helping paint every room, after first scrubbing the walls down with trisodium, which removed smoke odors; laundering clothing, bed linens, drapery; and cleaning the floors.

The day before she was born, Mike and I got a babysitter for Michael, Michelle, and Julie and went fishing off a pier on Lake Mendota. I remember thinking to myself, *Was it just five years ago when Mike proposed to me on a beach not far from here? Wow!*

Mary was born June 8. I originally planned on naming her Lisa Marie, but changed my mind because of Mike's mother's death almost six months earlier on December 25 of 1962. Her name was Frances, so named our daughter Mary Frances in her honor.

*   *   *

I would face another challenge in 1964. It was Sabin Sunday, a day in January designated to receive the polio vaccine. We returned home from the distribution site and were getting out of the car. While Mike helped the other kids, I carried six-month-old Mary. Our driveway was gravel with sunken two-by-fours along the edges. The boards must have been slippery from the snow, and as I got out of the car, I felt myself going down. All I could think of was Mary and her safety. I held her close to me and down I went, my left leg twisting.

I heard my leg bones crack, followed by excruciating pain worse than any I experienced during childbirth. The ambulance came and I remember the attendant telling me about a brand-new device they would be putting on my leg, an airbag, which helped immobilize the fracture. X-rays showed a spiral fracture extending between my knee and ankle. My leg was put in a full-length cast, a cast I would have for six months. I called the cast "Lucille," and my husband St. Michael the Archangel. The day I came home from the hospital, the kids all had vomiting and diarrhea. He did non-stop laundry, cooking, childcare, and taking care of me, including some personal care. I could write a book about those six months, and what one can do if they have to, including a chapter on having sex while in a full-length leg cast.

I couldn't carry little Mary, but I could hold her once I sat down. I placed a chair by her crib, and would sit on that chair when I'd do her diaper changes, or lift her out of the crib. She would then have to crawl to the kitchen or living room. It took a little coaxing at first, but she caught on.

One day, Julie, who was two, was doing something she wasn't supposed to be doing and I told her I'd be taking her to her room for time out. I was lying on the couch and I noticed she scanned the room and then blurted out, "You can't take me to my room because you don't have your crutches." Her eyes tripled in size as I got off the couch and hopped on one foot toward her. She realized at that point that I was *disabled* but *able*.

In the spring, I planted my entire garden by sliding along boards placed between the rows, my leg wrapped with a dry-cleaner plastic bag.

By the end of July, before my cast was removed, I could run with my crutches.

*   *   *

It was June of 1967 and I was relaxing in a lawn chair at a campsite, stopping for a moment from writing in my travel journal to gaze at a mountain stream making its way over and around rocks, composing its own orchestral sound. It confirmed the decision Mike and I made to purchase a Trailblazer camper as a less expensive way to take vacations with our children, who were then ages four to eight. I had never traveled farther than Wisconsin and Illinois so was savoring every aspect of the trip.

When we entered the Smoky Mountains to register for our campsite, I was mesmerized with the natural fog that looked like large smoke plumes from the distance. I lay on my back in a grassy spot, trying to take it all in, much to the delight of the kids.

One morning Mike had taken the four kids for a hike, leaving me alone with my thoughts. My eyes were closed and I was listening to the pleasant sound of the water, the bird sounds in the forest, distant chatter of other campers, and began thinking of my mother who had such an appreciation of nature.

Mom, it has been some time since I've had an imaginary talk with you. I feel in my heart and soul that you are alive somewhere. As time goes by my greatest fear is that your calming voice and beautiful face will fade from my memory. I look at the last photo I took of you on June 1, 1952, the day before you left, knowing you would've changed after fifteen years. I wonder if you still purse your lips and blow upward to resettle a wisp of hair that has made its way down your forehead and across your eye. You said in the letter you sent shortly after you left that your dark hair turned snow white. Would I know you if I saw you?

Your babies are not babies anymore and I have babies of my own, four of them, and they are growing so fast. I'm sure you are acutely aware of our ages, especially the way you loved celebrating birthdays. How I loved watching you design frosting flowers for the cakes without benefit of fancy equipment, just tightly rolled wax paper cones filled with frosting and you squeezing with just enough pressure. The best part for us kids was licking off the wax paper when you were finished.

Susan was married in 1965 to a man named Bruce Rieber and they have two children, Kim and Daniel. Susan first met Bruce at the orphanage. Bruce comes from a large family and has two parents but for reasons I don't know, was in the orphanage for a short time.

*Rita will be married this month at the cathedral in La
Crosse and our little Michelle will be the flower girl. Her
husband-to-be, Calvin, is from Bangor, Maine, where they
will live. His plan is to follow in his grandfather and father's
footsteps and join the police force.*

*Mary graduated from St. Mary's School of Nursing in
1961, is single, and working in Florida.*

*Fred is making a career in the Air Force, and currently is
serving in Vietnam. He is married and will be living in
Ogden, Utah, when he returns home in November of this year.
His wife's name is Alice and they do not have any children.*

*Barbara attends the University of Wisconsin in Madison
and is studying to be a recreational therapist. It's nice
having her in Madison as I get to see her once in a while.
I am able to see Patricia as well. She graduated from high
school this year, is sharing an apartment with two other
girls, and working at Central Colony which is an institution
for children with disabilities. Her apartment is only about
fifteen minutes from us.*

*Dad lives with Aunt Mabel when he isn't on a painting
assignment. He does his best to keep in touch. Any letter
we write doesn't go unanswered. Mike and I try to visit or
have them both at our home when possible. Dad doesn't talk
much, or I should say at all, about…*

"Mom, Mom!"

"I want to tell her."

"No, I want to."

*Mom, I need to go. Mike is back with the kids and they sure
sound excited about something. Love you.*

"OK, tell me about your walk, but one at a time. Let's
start with Mary."

"Mom," chimed the three oldest, disappointed at not
being first.

"We walked on water!"

"You did what?"

Before Mary could answer, Julie piped up in her confident voice, "It was so much fun. I wasn't even scared."

Knowing how timid Michelle was around water, I was eager to hear her story.

"Did you walk in a stream?"

"No, on top of a waterfall, but Daddy held my hand. I had to take off my shoes. The water was cold and tickled my toes."

I looked up at Mike in disbelief. He just smiled.

"I was the first one across," boasted Michael, our oldest. "We have to go back so you can do it."

"Let me think about it while I make some lunch for you. You must be starved after such an adventure."

I went inside our trailer and made up some macaroni and cheese while Mike made a fire so the kids could roast hotdogs. They loved doing that, but it was no small feat to end up with a nicely cooked hotdog, versus hotdog ala ashes or blackened hotdog. It didn't matter, as there was something magical about sitting at a picnic table in nature's dining room, the smell of the campfire smoke intermingling with mountain air, best appreciated by closing one's eyes and taking a deep breath through your nose.

We ate and put everything away as there were bears in the Smoky Mountains. We had already seen bear on one of our drives through the park. Of course, the kids wanted to get out of the car, but that was a no-no. However, I was able to take photos from the car window.

We doused the fire and, with camera around my neck, I was led by four excited children and a husband to *the waterfall.*

As we walked the path through the forest I had to chuckle as I observed little Mary, the four-year-old, frequently stopping, her body bent over looking at a leaf, or a pretty rock, or pointing out an insect. It brought back memories of one day at home when she came to me from outside, her little hand closed, and said, "I want you to see my friend." She slowly opened her hand and there was a ladybug.

I looked up at Mike and voiced my gratitude for this vacation. He agreed.

I couldn't believe it when the path ended abruptly. To continue on the path, you had to cross the waterfall, which looked to be about eight feet across with a six-foot drop. While I was looking it over, the kids already had their shoes off and were on the other side, even Michelle.

"Come on, Mom."

It seems so silly now but my legs felt rubbery as I crossed, holding Mike's hand, or I should say, Mike almost pulling me across, and saying, "Look up toward the stream, not at the drop-off."

"You did it, Mom. You did it."

*   *   *

A few days later we were back in Wisconsin getting ready for my sister Rita's wedding. While we were on vacation Julie Motzko, a backyard neighbor and excellent seamstress, was sewing Michelle's flower girl dress. On our return, I had to take Michelle for final fittings.

Julie was from Germany, and her personality had the presence of a 50-foot ocean wave. She not only sewed, but had gardens in which a weed would not dare to appear. She told me she had sewn as long as she could remember. As a little girl she'd pick up scraps of fabric from her mother's sewing projects and hand-sew clothes for her dolls.

Julie wasn't much older than I, but I could talk to her in almost a daughter to mother fashion about raising children (she had a daughter, Cindy), cooking, and sewing. I don't know how she did it—as busy as she was, her kitchen always was filled with the most wonderful aromas, whether it was soup simmering on a burner or coffeecake in the oven. I usually came home with a sample or a recipe. Julie remained a lifelong friend.

The day of the wedding, as I looked at my beautiful little daughter and my radiant sister, I so wished Mom was there. Rita most resembled Mom and I was picturing them standing side by side smiling at each other.

I held back my feelings of sadness the best I could but I dreaded the thought of another sibling moving away. Rita and Cal would be living in Bangor, Maine. Life has a way of moving on, I guess, in order to keep one busy so you don't dwell on missing family.

Michelle was a Brownie in Girl Scouts and also attended dance classes. Michael was in Boy Scouts and was chosen by his fellow Cub Scouts to be the denner of his troop. A denner held the flag when the Pledge of Allegiance was recited and also assisted the den mother.

I passed a state exam for a head nurse position at Central Wisconsin Center where I was employed. Working the day shift Monday through Friday gave me more quality time with my family.

*   *   *

Before the 1960s ended, Rita and Cal would have a son, Calvin, and a daughter, Tamara. Patricia was married to Robert

Jones, November 16, 1968, and had their first child, Robin, in 1969.

My mother's father, Damian Debovik, died October 15, 1968. He was a wonderful grandfather with a gentle spirit. I wished he would've had answers about her disappearance before he passed away. Mike and I went to Chicago to attend his funeral. During the service Mike whispered to me, "Who are you looking for?"

"What?" I whispered back.

"You keep turning your head as if you're looking for someone."

It was like I felt Mom's presence in the church.

Chapter 21
The Seventies, Eighties, and Nineties

Mike and I had two more sons: Mark William born April 24, 1970, and David Ashley born December 13, 1976. I loved being a mother, and each birth was as much a miracle as the first. I had a miscarriage in February 1978 and was devastated. The little one would have been named Eric Matthew or Lisa Marie.

On June 6, 1970, my sister, Mary, married Larry Simonis. She chose to have both her foster father, Larry Alland, *and* Dad walk her down the aisle. Dad was of average height, but on that day, he was six feet tall.

We moved to a larger home with more space for our growing family in 1972. With four bedrooms, it was easier to accommodate my dad when he would come for longer visits. Dad enjoyed his visits even with the bustling activity of our children. He would comment, "When I return home, the silence is deafening."

We lived in that home for sixteen years, years filled with memories of David's birth in 1976, our children's teenage to adult years, Michelle joining the Armed Services, Mary venturing off to Anchorage, Alaska, followed by Scott, the love of her life, with subsequent marriage in 1983, our son Michael and our daughter Julie's marriages, grandchildren, surprise birthday parties, family reunions, and all the other things that make a house, a home.

It wasn't *all* happiness; we dealt with teenage experimentation of drugs and alcohol. A magnet I've had on my refrigerator for 46 years reads: *There is no such thing as a problem, only a challenge waiting to be solved.* We raised our children with good moral values and example, and because of that and trust in God, I felt they would find their way back if they strayed off the path.

As the years passed I tried to visualize what Mom might look like. I got some sense of this when I visited Aunt Isabel, Mom's sister. Sometimes I would see Mom in my dreams, but she always looked like I last saw her.

When I turned 36 in 1973, my mom's age when she left, I tried putting myself in her shoes. When she was 36 there were seven of us, ages three to fifteen. When I was 36, I had five children, ages three to fourteen. With the flickering of 36 candles and my family singing *Happy Birthday* to me, I had a smile on my face, but silently was asking the question: *What would be so bad that I would want to leave them—another man, abuse, mental illness…? I couldn't imagine walking out the door and not looking back. What kind of pain accompanied Mom's decision to leave?*

My sister, Barbara, was the last of us girls to be married. She married Woodrow Hilleque on June 28, 1974. I especially missed my mom during these special events of our lives, as well as during the sad times, such as November 1978. It was the year Dad decided not to be with us for Thanksgiving. He usually came for the holidays, especially after his sister, Mabel, died in 1971. Maybe he had a premonition. My Mike deer hunted north of where Dad lived and would pick him up on his way home.

The irony of the story is that my sister, Mary, and her husband, Larry and children traveled to La Crosse from Madison to spend Thanksgiving with Larry's folks. They had planned on stopping in New Lisbon to see Dad and show him their two-month-old baby, Scott. Holiday traffic, along with a blinding snow storm, forced them to make the decision to stop and see Dad on the way back home. When they came to the house, they found Dad lying on the floor, his uneaten breakfast on the table. The medical examiner ruled he had died of a massive heart attack. He was 69.

When Mary called, my emotions ran the gamut. *I wish he could've found out what happened to Mom, and, with the benefit of hindsight, I wish I would've asked more questions about why he thought she left. My children just lost their last grandparent, unless Mom is still alive. They will miss him so much, and his letters. When they wrote to him, an answer was guaranteed.*

David, our two-year-old, sensed something was wrong when I began to cry. He wrapped his little arms around my legs. How does one tell a two-year-old about the death of a grampa he adored, a grampa who called him "Little D"?

The rest of the kids were on Thanksgiving break and visibly upset over the sad news. The older ones stayed with David, while eight-year-old Mark went with me to New Lisbon so I could help with funeral arrangements. Mike and I would pass each other on the interstate as he was driving home from deer hunting. Mark asked many questions as we drove the 75 miles to New Lisbon: "What's a funeral? What will they do with Grampa?" I explained visitation, and how his grampa would be in a casket.

"What's a casket?"

"It's a fancy bed. Grampa will look like he is sleeping. His family and friends will stop in front of the casket, and they will talk and remember special things about him."

"Then what?"

"After the funeral he will be buried."

"In the ground?"

It was difficult for him to think of his grampa being in the ground. How does one explain about the body in the ground and the soul in heaven?

Father Mark Walljasper conducted a beautiful funeral Mass for our dad. As part of the service I read a poem, which Dad kept on a stand next to his chair in the living room:

> **I Needed the Quiet**
> I needed the quiet, so He took me aside
> Into the shadows where we could confide;
> Away from the bustle, where all the day long,
> I hurried and worried when active and strong.
>
> I needed the quiet, though at first I rebelled,
> But gently, so gently, the cross He upheld,
> And whispered so sweetly of spiritual things.
> Though weakened in body, my spirit took wings,
> To heights never dreamed of when active and gay,
> He loved me so greatly He drew me away.
>
> I needed the quiet, no prison, my bed,
> But a beautiful valley of blessing instead,
> A place to grow richer, in Jesus to hide—
> I needed the quiet, so He took me aside.
> *Author Unknown*

*   *   *

Thinking of Mom was a daily ritual, especially after my dad's death. I would have one-sided conversations. *Are you alive? Are you well? Do you have someone to love? Do you know I have never stopped thinking of you?* Many of these thoughts came in the stillness of the night, after the lights were out, as I snuggled between the sheets.

In the 1980s, my sister Mary and I hired a detective with missing person experience to initiate a search for our mother. All we had to go on was the letter written by her in 1952 postmarked Elgin, Illinois. The focal point was area restaurants. Mom loved to cook and had worked part-time in restaurants, mainly truck stops, when she was still with us. Thirty years had passed but it was all we had. The detective did a search using her social security number to no avail.

A woman in Elgin who knew our mother thought she remembered her moving "somewhere" out west. We didn't obtain any personal information, which was disappointing, but we tried. At the time of our investigation Mom would have been 67 years old and time seemed to be running out. We still had HOPE, although at times I felt hope was as futile as stitching stones together.

*   *   *

Our first grandchild, Michael Lee, was born June 25, 1983. I was at a nurses' get-together in La Crosse, Wisconsin and staying at a mom-and-pop motel without a phone in the room, and of course, this was before cell phones. Before I left for the evening, I asked the manager if my son, Michael, or his wife, Nancy, could call the motel if the baby was born, and if she would leave a note on my door to let me know. I returned to the motel about eleven and was overjoyed to see motel stationery taped to the door with the note: *Congratulations, you have a grandson.* The hardest part was not having anyone to share the news with. I cried tears of joy, readied myself for bed, said a prayer of thanks, and thought of my mom: *Mom, I'm a grandma, and you are a great-grandmother.*

Later in the summer, Mike and I went to Europe for a month. Our daughter, Michelle, was stationed at an army base in Stuttgart, Germany so the trip was two-fold. We met her in Frankfurt for a few hours prior to our train trip to

Warsaw, Poland, with plans to have her join us ten days later. It was quite the experience traveling to Poland by train as we had to pass through East Germany. When we reached the border of East Germany, during the middle of the night, the train stopped, border guards came into the train and went car to car with flashlights checking passports. Officers with dogs pulling tightly against their leashes stood outside. I've often wondered about a young man who was put off the train that night, for reasons I do not know. Mike and I thought we would be in the same sleeper car but had been separated by the conductor when we boarded. I remember thinking, *I hope we meet up in the morning.*

We visited the countries of Poland, Germany, Switzerland, Belgium, the Netherlands, and France. My dad's family was from Germany and Switzerland, and my mom's from Poland and Belo-Russia, making it special for me. Later in our lifetime we were able to visit the countries of Mike's ancestry, Norway and Ireland.

In the late 1980s, after fireman were no longer required to live in Madison, we moved out of the city to a home across the street from Lake Wisconsin, eight miles from Sauk City. Mike retired about a year later.

The house on the lake would be the house some of our grandchildren would remember. When we moved, our last two children at home were Mark, eighteen, and David, twelve. We had been blessed with seven grandchildren: Michael, Jennifer, Brianna, Carrie, Tyler, Derek, and Jacob. Our daughter, Michelle, and Joe married in 1992, and our son, Mark, and Kala in 1994. There were six more grandchildren by the time we moved from this home: Trevor, Christina, Chelsea, Jared, Michela, Sierra, and Cameron. They enjoyed riding on the pontoon boat especially if we were going to the ice cream shop along the shores of Merrimac, or taking a ride on the Merrimac Ferry across Lake Wisconsin. One Christmas, their gifts were life-jackets.

Cameron, the son of Mark and Kala, would have a sister, Hannah, in 1998. Hannah had distinction of being the youngest of the grandchildren for twelve years. Our son, David, and Stacy were married in 2010 and have two children, Lyla and Naomi, making our grand total of grand-children, seventeen.

The year we moved I took a position at Sauk Prairie Me-morial Hospital where I worked until my retirement in 2001. The hospital had an awesome reimbursement program if one wished to go on to school, so in 1991, at age fifty-four, I enrolled at the University of Wisconsin-Madison to obtain my BSN (Bachelor of Science in Nursing). Because I contin-ued to work, I went to school part-time and graduated in May 1996, along with three of my co-workers. It was great being on campus as older adults. The media doesn't concen-trate on the many fine young people, yes, even the students with purple hair or earrings in their tongues expressing an identity. Connie, Pam, Karen, (my co-workers and fellow classmates) and I were sometimes regarded as their college moms. Going back to school was one of the highlights in my life. Another highlight was being called a *nerd* by our son, David, when I complained about a grade of A-minus.

In April 1996, we moved to Wisconsin Dells. It wasn't that we didn't like our lake home, but we both had the desire to live in a log home. Our home was 36 miles from my job, but traffic was light at 5:30 in the morning, and the 45-minute drive home at the end of the day was let-down time after a busy day at the hospital. The final reward was arriving to the seclusion of our wooded property, beautiful no matter the season. I took many walks, alone with my thoughts, knowing as more and more years passed, I most likely would not get answers about my mom.

In May 1998, I was taking a shower and doing my monthly breast exam. Disbelief went through my mind when I felt a pea-size lump above my left nipple. I made the decision not to tell Mike. He was looking forward to a week of fishing with his friends, Ralph, Tom, and Tom, and would be leaving in a couple of days. When I went to Mass on Sunday I had a difficult time concentrating on the service. All I could think of was the lump. After church my friend, Deanna, and I went to a flower garden. I can forget almost anything when surrounded by plants.

Mike and I spent about an hour together before the guys picked him up for fishing the following morning. It was a beautiful morning and everything seemed special, not knowing what this lump was going to mean in our lives. After he left I called and made an appointment. I was seen the same day and had a mammogram. The next day while at work, X-Ray staff called saying I needed an ultrasound. The ultrasound showed mammographic changes and a breast biopsy was scheduled for May 21 and confirmed carcinoma.

I shared the news with Mike when he returned home on the 23rd, and then with the rest of the family, as well as my staff. I welcomed the prayers and support, although I was providing support, especially for my family; it was difficult for them.

The following was written in my diary on June 5:

The news of my cancer is devastating to our children. Michael is feeling guilty about past sins. How can I assure him that he didn't cause my cancer. He is such a good man

and son. Michelle—wishing she lived closer. Julie—sensi-
tive. "Mom, there is so much I need to share with you yet."
Mary—heartbroken. Mark—so concerned and yet afraid.
David—sad and feeling very alone in Colorado. We will
survive this.

On June 9, I had a mastectomy but did not need chemo-therapy.

There was another note in my diary written Tuesday, June 16:

Had a rough night. Everything hurt—drain site, had a head-
ache, body stiffness. Woke up at 2 a.m. feeling very sorry
for myself. Cried a few tears, got it back together, read some
poetry and fell back to sleep.

I had another entry written at 05:45 a.m. on Wednesday, June 17:

Had a super night. Slept well with only potty breaks to in-
terrupt my sleep. Mike just left to go fishing with Mark. He
deserves the day off and I know I will be OK here by myself. It
is a beautiful morning. The woodpecker is rat-a-tatting with
an accompaniment of song from the other birds. The sun is
gently peeking through the trees.

I mention the above entries because I would learn in 2011 that my mom died at 5:00 a.m. on June 17, 1998, of lung cancer.

I am a positive person, but the experience of having cancer made me more appreciative of family and friends, my environment, and things as simple as watching a caterpillar about which I wrote a poem:

Lessons I learned in the Garden

I am a breast cancer survivor
Gardening is therapy.
Kneeling down in my garden
I realize I am not alone.
There is a caterpillar on a mission.
I watch.

In undulating movements
he makes his way up a plant stem,
inch by inch, by inch.
I watch.

Crawling onto just the right leaf,
he waits, waits for his weight to
slowly lower him to a neighboring plant.
I watch.

He journeys down the stem.
His tiny feet like marching soldiers,
raising his head up so far,
he is almost erect, looking, looking.
I watch.

A wide blade of grass protruding
into the plant seems to beckon him,
stretching, stretching, almost
dangling in space, he reaches it.

I am in awe.
I glance at my watch. An hour has passed.
I am still on my knees, garden trowel in hand.
Patience, determination, perseverance.
Lessons learned in the garden.

I received first-place recognition for this poem at the 2013
Writer's Conference in Madison, Wisconsin.

I would be diagnosed with cancer in the other breast in 2004 and have my second mastectomy, but I'm here and life is good.

Chapter 22
Being a Sister Instead of a Mother

It was October of 2001. Mike and I were visiting my sister, Rita, and her husband, Alex, in Toronto, Ontario. I had retired from nursing in April, and was enjoying the freedom of traveling without time restrictions. Mike had retired from the fire department twelve years earlier. We had just returned from a month-long trip to Australia and New Zealand.

While in Toronto, I received a call from my sister, Mary, in Green Bay, Wisconsin, telling me she had fallen from a ladder while painting her upstairs bathroom, necessitating an ambulance ride to the emergency room, and her leg immobilized. Since her husband was a long-distance truck driver during the week, her plan was to go to Florida and stay at her foster mother's home for six weeks.

However, at an appointment with an orthopedist, she learned she had a tibial plateau fracture (a fracture of the shin bone). On October 30 she had surgery with placement of nine internal screws, and an order for no ambulation. Going to Florida was not an option so she asked if I'd be able to stay with her Monday through Friday. Larry would be home on weekends. Mike and I talked it over and felt it would work out for me to make that commitment. My Mike could cook and clean, so I knew without a doubt he could manage.

I packed my bags and arrived in Green Bay two and a half hours later. I pulled in the driveway and parked at the back of the house. I got out of the car, grabbed my bags, and knocked at the back door. Gypsy, the family dog, readily greeted me. I opened the door a crack and announced my arrival. I heard Mary say, "Come in. I'm in the family room."

There she was, lying in a bed that had been placed in the family room, leg elevated, and a look that said, "I can't believe this happened."

I set my suitcase down, and gave her a gentle hug, "Mary, Mary. You sure know how to do it up right."

Larry was quick to thank me for coming.

I remember sitting on the edge of the couch waiting for my instructions, like a new person for hire.

I was at her house about one and a half weeks when we decided I could care for her at my home until she had to return to Green Bay for ongoing physical therapy, and then I would stay for as long as necessary. Her daughter, Rebecca, came from Madison and picked up the dog. On November 16 we loaded–and I mean loaded–my little PT Cruiser with luggage, pillows, walker, and anything else we thought we might need. Mary was sandwiched in the middle of it all.

Mary may have been non-ambulatory but it didn't slow her down; where there was a will, there was a way. We Christmas shopped; we visited my son David in Eau Claire, Wisconsin, for his 25th birthday, and my daughter Julie on her 40th; and experienced the handicap accessible world, *or not.*

On one of our shopping trips things were going well; Mary had a motorized cart with a large attached basket in which to place her items. The aisles were wide enough, and I could reach merchandise for her on high shelves. We needed to make a restroom stop. As we approached the area we saw a sign read: *No Items can be Taken into Restroom.* I went and checked with store personnel to see if there was an exception if one had a motorized cart.

"I don't think so," was the answer.

We unloaded our items onto the floor, hoping a diligent employee wouldn't come by and put the items back on the shelves. Then the fun began—we had to make three sharp turns to get *into* the bathroom only to find the handicap-accessible space was at the *end* of the row. I waited outside the door in case Mary needed help. She wheeled herself out, washed her hands, looked around for the paper towels—even with her arms extended, they were out of reach. We stood there and laughed.

Once Mary's therapy sessions started, I stayed with her in Green Bay, Monday through Friday until April 1, a period of three months. Those three months with her would be the most time we had spent together since we were kids, and before Mom left in 1952.

We had many memorable moments, such as decorating her artificial Christmas tree not only for Christmas, but for Valentine's Day, Saint Patrick's Day, and Easter. We had our scheduled cleaning day, grocery shopping day, rented movie nights, and make-up application sessions—I frightened a realtor when I answered a knock at the door, my face caked with a white beauty mask, "You'll have to come back another time." (Mary and Larry were making plans to downsize.)

We enjoyed just being sisters. In fact, one day when we were enjoying a cup of tea, Mary gave me permission to just be a sister and not a *mother*. I would be reminded of that again in 2004 by my sisters, Susan and Patricia. It sounded like I had been committed to my role as substitute mother; I'm pleased I left that impression.

We had our serious moments, too. I was surprised during one of our conversations when I mentioned Mom, and she said, "I don't want to talk about her." I respected her wishes but brought it up a few days later as I helped her get positioned for an afternoon rest. "Mary, I didn't realize you had the feelings you do about Mom."

She gave me that questioning Steinmetz glance: stop, stare, wait. We all have it. "Rose, I'm sorry, but your bringing up Mom in conversations is something I'm not comfortable hearing. It's too painful for me and not talking about her is my way of coping." *I probably did bring her up often. I didn't have a foster mother to talk about; I just had Mom, someone I loved and missed very much.* Mary talked about anxiety attacks when she went into foster care and how her foster mom lovingly helped her through those times.

I sat down in a nearby chair. "Mary, according to Mom's letter, she was afraid when Dad was drinking."

She spoke with sadness in her voice, "I remember the night we heard Mom and Dad fighting , and she ran outside and hid in the woods."

I closed my eyes for a moment visualizing Mom and Dad.

"Mary, I'll never forget it. I was shocked when I came downstairs and saw Mom's face. I'd never seen him be mean to Mom. Freddie told me he snuck outside that night and sat with her until she felt safe coming back into the house—probably after Dad fell asleep. Maybe there were things going on we didn't even know about."

"But how can a mother leave her babies?"

"I've asked the same question over and over, but I know she loved us; she said in her letter she thought about coming back after three weeks, but was afraid of going to prison for abandonment. I recall asking the detective we hired in the '80s if Mom's impression was right, and he said in the 1950s that would have been true."

Mary stroked the area of her fracture.

"Are you having pain?"

"No, I'm OK."

"Mary, you were so close to Dad. Things may have been different if they'd had counseling. All I know is there was something special in our upbringing, something deep that we inherited from both Mom and Dad, and our grandparents."

"I'm going to rest now."

"Mary, thanks for sharing. I don't know what the seven of us would have been like if Mom hadn't left, but our bond is beautiful."

"I agree."

In further conversations we were able to discuss our memories and feelings and came to accept how we were affected and how we coped in different ways. It was a moment in time.

Chapter 23
The Sisters' Journey
as Written in My Travel Journal

Thursday, April 29, 2004

Our journey is about to begin for the sister week in Toronto. Mary arrived about 2 pm, Barbara at 3 pm, and Susan and her husband John at 5:45 pm. My Mike, and Susan's John, will be the send-off team in the morning.

We sat down to a supper of beef stew, coleslaw, and bread. You could feel the excitement between us girls, and already tears of joy emerging. We were engaged in lots of chatting. It is hard to believe what it will be like when all six of us girls are sitting together in the living room of our sister Rita's apartment.

Amtrak departs at 11:45 am tomorrow. Our sister Patricia has already flown to Toronto.

Friday, April 30, 2004

Mike prepared us a delectable bacon and egg breakfast. After breakfast there was much scurrying around getting last-minute things together.

We arrived at the Wisconsin Dells train station, took photos, and chatted with the station master. Sue even helped the stationmaster wrap a gift. When the train arrived and we boarded, the conductor informed us we would not be able to get four seats together until we reached Milwaukee. We conversed and read. Arrived in Chicago, Illinois at 3:45 pm. Chicago Union Station was extremely busy with commuters scurrying everywhere. I can't believe I have already used the word scurrying twice. It is what it is.

We got our bearings, inquired about the departure gate, and with three hours until departure we scouted out a place to dine in the Union Station food emporium. We chose the Snuggery Bar, ordered refreshments and talked until time to board the Lake Shore Limited.

Saturday, May 1, 2004
Sleep was sporadic during the night as we were trying to stay comfortable, and interruptions due to passengers boarding at different stops. Arrived in Buffalo, New York at 6:40 am. As part of our itinerary we planned on seeing Niagara Falls, not far from Buffalo. We were happy to find out that we could take a taxi to Niagara without returning to the city of Buffalo to get back on the train. We could depart from Niagara.

We arrived in Niagara, stored our luggage in lockers, ate breakfast, and visited the Niagara Casino for an hour. No riches. We then booked a ride on the "Maid of the Mist" boat to view Niagara Falls up close and personal. It was misty and windy but it did not dampen our spirits or the beauty of the falls.

We dined at Ruby Tuesdays. I had a great lunch of tilapia, broccoli, and creamy mashed cauliflower. While eating, the sun came out which prompted my sister Mary and me to walk to the lookout for another view of Niagara Falls, and oh what a view. While taking pictures, we met a lovely family from Columbia, who now live in Toronto. I was able to make some conversation with the woman in my broken Spanish, but it worked.

It has been a spectacular day and we are not even in Toronto yet. We are now sitting in the Canada Rail station, or I should say, some of us are sitting. Barbara is reading, and Susan and Mary are stretched out on a wooden bench catching some shuteye. It is 4:15 pm and we depart at 5:45 pm.

The ride from Niagara went rather quickly to Toronto. Before I go on I must write how Sue almost gave us heart fright. Shortly after we boarded the train but before we left, she discovered she did not have her purse. She bolted off the train and luckily found her purse on the bench. Upon returning to the train she couldn't find her ticket. The ticket somehow ended up on the floor, two seats ahead. We laughed and teased her a lot, and then heard her say, "Whose ticket is that lying in the aisle?" It was mine. It had slipped out of my pocket.

We proceeded to the dining car, actually a small snack bar, and bought sandwiches.

As we were passing Hamilton, Ontario, we received a phone call from our sister, Rita. She was asking how close we were to Toronto, and telling us that she and her husband, Alex, and our sister, Patricia, were anxiously waiting for our arrival.

As we approached Toronto, we each pinned a large pink bow to our clothing. It was our way of saying, as we came off the train, "Happy Birthday to Rita [May 6th) and Patricia (May 10th)."

We hugged, kissed, jumped for joy, and then trekked thru Union Station. There was nary an elevator to be found. We pulled our luggage up steps, balanced luggage on the escalator, and pulled it some more before arriving at Rita and Alex's apartment on the harbor front bordering Lake Ontario. I never tire of looking out of their windows; sailboats, ships, harbor tour boats on the lake, sounds of traffic and sirens on the streets below, and the movement of people in the apartments across the way. It's quite a change from the peace and serenity of my rural surroundings.

We snacked on cheese, grapes, nuts, and wine, made plans for Sunday Mass, and left the apartment at 10 PM. Patricia was staying at Rita and Alex's and the rest of us were booked at the Radisson Hotel across the street. We unpacked, took our showers, and all collapsed. We were so tired.

Sunday, May 2, 2004

Up at about 8 am—a rainy, gray day. Enjoyed a great breakfast at Rita's. Cameras were clicking. I think this will be a given all week.

I handed out to each of my sisters a book called, IN PRAISE AND CELEBRATION OF SISTERS by Helen Exely. I asked how they would feel about each of us writing a message in each other's books. They agreed. I also gave each of them a whimsical figurine. "The Girls" figurines were as follows:

Myself—The Gardener

Mary—The Cheerleader—she loves the Packers

Susan—The Gambler—loves bingo and slots

Barbara—The Shopper—loves to find a good deal

Rita—The Diner—loves a fine meal

Patricia—The Fisher person—lives in Alaska and loves to catch salmon

Patricia then handed us gifts. She gave us a see-thru bag filled with a crystal heart, a pewter box, and small wooden cutouts of moose, bear, stars, pine trees, and boats.

Rita gave each of us a kitchen towel.

After oohs and ahs, and thank yous, we left the apartment and took the transit system to St. Michael's Cathedral. It was so special having the six of us at Mass. It was hard keeping back the tears. Our brother, Fred, so much wanted to come to Toronto as well but just couldn't coordinate flight arrangements with time off from work. We thought of him often. After Mass we took a tour of the cathedral. The cathedral was built in 1845, and Gothic in style. It has the largest stained-glass window in North America. The tour was informative and worthwhile.

We then went to the Bata Shoe Museum and spent a couple of hours there. My impression was, women have loved their shoes for a very long time.

Our perfect day was climaxed by a great ham supper pre-
pared by Rita. After supper we laughed until we ached watching
Mr. Bean videos. Mr. Bean is a comedic fellow from England. Mr.
Bean was a new experience for Patricia and Barbara. Our supper
was well settled after all the laughter.

We readied ourselves and went to Rita's apartment for
breakfast. The outdoor temperature was 36 degrees. We spent a
good amount of time around the dining room table recalling our
memories of childhood, the orphanage, foster home experiences,
and personal stories. We laughed, we cried, and agreed, in spite
of adversity, we all were blessed in many ways, and have an
unbreakable bond.

This beautiful cleansing of our souls was followed by a stroll
thru the Toronto Music Garden, a garden designed thru the col-
laboration of a horticulturist, an architect, and Yo Yo Ma, a vio-
linist. Alex joined the six of us, which was a brave move. What
fun we had. We danced around the maypole, took photos, enjoyed
the beauty of the golden-yellow daffodils, multi-colored tulips,
airy pasque flowers, and the budding shrubs and trees. Of par-
ticular interest, was a tree called European larch (larix decidua).
Two men who maintain the garden informed me this tree would
grow in Zone 4. The pine needles on the tree looked like little
bow ties along the stem, and the emerging pinecones were a dark
pink. Stunning!

We passed a telephone booth as we walked along the harbor
front, and within minutes we simultaneously came up with the
idea of seeing if the six of us could wedge ourselves into the booth.
We did it and Alex took a photo to prove it.

We returned to the apartment for lunch before going on a
Harbor Boat tour. I had previously been on the tour but learned
new information. Our next stop was Queens Quay Mall. Bar-
bara purchased a new outfit to wear to the theater on Wednes-
day evening to see "Hairspray." Barbara is frugal when it comes

to buying new clothes, but what could she do with five sisters urging her on. Susan purchased black slacks and I a black tee. The best part of the shopping experience, was that it was the first time in our life that all six of us girls were shopping together—a priceless moment.

We had an interesting supper of bruschetta, cheese, and wine. We were going to watch more Mr. Bean tapes, but got caught up in conversation. I asked my sisters if they would mind sharing what they had written in the Sister books. It was an emotional purging. The messages written in my book were an affirmation of their appreciation of what I had done over the years to never lose our sense of family. It was one of the greatest gifts I ever received.

Following are the messages they wrote:

Rose,

Hasn't this just been the greatest adventure for all of us? We've learned of our special connections to each other thru the years and of the many threads (sometimes fine) that have held our life's tapestry together. Much of the time you were the needle, pulling the threads tight. This week we celebrate our survival, our love, our bond, and our sisterhood, and like Patricia and Bob's sculpture, our lives share one bright center of light. I have been blessed having you as a sis who cherishes family, nature, and life, and one that I know is fun to be with. Bless you, and you are loved. Mary

Rose,

Thank you for the love and strength to keep our family always in touch. You have always been there for me in good times and bad. I know I would never have made it without you. Traveling with you to all those beautiful places has been a joy and twice as enjoyable. You are truly a beautiful and caring person and I am so blessed to have you as my sister. This '6 Sister's Week' has refreshed my family soul. Thank you for YOU. Your sis, Sue

Rose,

You are the mother we 'lost' too soon. Thank you for reeling us all back in when we were separated. There has been warmth extended to me, which I never felt in my foster home. Thank you and bless you. Barb

Rose,

Seeing you on arrival at the train station, your bright face, smile, and the biggest pink ribbon attached to your shoulder in honor of my birthday, filled my eyes with tears and my heart burst with joy. I felt a flashback from birth to present. You have always been my rock to ground me, and branches to surround me with unending love and support. I felt what only sisters can feel when together, a happiness that makes the heart too big for the body. I love you. Rita

Rose,

I hope you know you are so special to me. You keep our family, A FAMILY. I thank you for this above ALL else. Through all our ups and downs you have been the BIG SISTER to always support us. I hope you know we are also there for you. I thank you for your LOVE. Your baby sister, Patricia

We ended our beautiful day by joining hands in a circle of love and respect and said our goodnights. Mary, Sue, Barbara, and I felt a void without Patricia and Rita when we returned to the Radisson for the night.

Tuesday, May 4, 2004

Today was a workday for Rita, her only workday during our visit. Alex took the week off, which I think was generous of him. After breakfast, Alex and we girls went to the Antique Market on the harbor front. Patricia purchased a bronze bust of a woman. We browsed awhile and headed for First Canadian Place, where Rita's workplace was located. Eve, Rita's boss, was touched emotionally by the fact all six of us girls were having a week together. Rita joined us for lunch at a Greek restaurant.

Following lunch we worked our way home via the underground district. An entire mall complex is under the city.

Another stop was at the CN Tower. Mary and I were the only ones that went to the top. The tower is 1815 feet tall. The top has a sway of 6 feet in both directions. The day was sunny and clear so you could see forever from the lookout area. We stretched out in a supine position on the glass floor and took photos of each other. It gives one an illusion that you are free falling since you can see down to the base of the tower. We then went to the Sky-pod, which was another thirty-three stories up. What a surprise when we exited the building and found Patricia, Sue, and Barb still waiting for us. We had been in the tower for an hour. Alex had walked back to the apartment because his daughter, Sandie, was coming to do a photo shoot of us girls upon our return. Photos were taken in the Radisson and out of doors. She informed us they would be black and white. I will be eager to get them.

We had a birthday supper tonight to celebrate the birthdays of Rita and Patricia, which are not until the 6th and 10th, but Patricia flies back to Alaska tomorrow. Gifts were given, and we all agreed the days had flown by all too quickly. We closed the evening with a group hug and thanks for a special week.

Wednesday, May 5, 2004
Patricia flew back to Alaska today. We felt the void. We relaxed during the day, and this evening went to the Princess Theater to see the musical, "Hairspray". Barbara, looking so nice in her new outfit, had a bloody nose during the performance, adding some unwanted detail to her new duds.

The above entry was the final entry in my travel journal. I believe it was Friday, May 7, when we returned by train to Wisconsin. I remember the train pulling into the Wisconsin Dells train station, and looking out the window, seeing Mike and John ready to greet us, and wondering to myself how I could put into words the depth of our sisters' journey.

Chapter 24
They Called Her "Mema"

O n May 25, 2011, my sister Patricia received a phone call from a young lady stating, "I believe Mema, I mean my great-grandmother, is your mother."

The way this unfolded, according to Patricia, was nine years earlier when she was doing genealogy research. She found family trees of a cousin and third cousin of ours, Art Lamberti and Marguerite Czajka. Information was shared between the three of them. Both Marguerite and Art had posted photos of our mom and her family. Sometime after the posting of photos, Art received an email from a Kim Wagner inquiring about Eleanor Olga Debovik (our mother). She stated a photo of a girl holding a kitty was her grandmother.

Art forwarded this email to Patricia. When she read it, she knew Mom must have had another child after she left us. Patricia emailed Kim many times, telling her about us, including names, addresses, and phone numbers, but without a response. We were frustrated feeling so close to possible answers, but not getting them.

In 2011, Patricia and her husband, Bob, were on their annual spring trip from their home in Big Lake, Alaska, to several states in the Lower Forty-eight visiting family and friends. The last stop was in Idaho. On May 24, Patricia was cleaning out her emails and came across one from Art saying, on his website, there was a girl named Kristina Wagner inquiring about our mother and family. She said she was a great-granddaughter of our Mom's. Because it concerned our immediate family, Art did not respond to the email but forwarded it to Patricia. Patricia immediately emailed Kristina to tell her she would be flying home the next day, arriving home at 5 p.m. and to please call. On May 25 at 5:15 p.m. the phone rang and, after talking for three hours, Patricia was absolutely sure the mystery of our mother was on the way to being solved. Patricia would later say, "God was behind this. Do wish He would have worked a little faster."

Patricia called me at 10:51 p.m. (a three-hour time difference), with the news. After I hung up the phone I sat on the edge of the bed in darkness, not sure of what I felt. Was it a dream? I'd waited so long for this moment. I remember asking Patricia before she hung up if she had notified our brother and sisters.

"Mike, Mike. Wake up. Patricia called with information about Mom." And then I collapsed into his arms and sobbed. "I'll never see Mom. She died of lung cancer in 1998. I'll never be able to tell her I never stopped loving her, to tell her our lives turned out OK, to tell her…, to hug her. Why?"

"How did she find out about your mom?"

"From a woman named, Kristina, who said she's my mom's great-granddaughter. She's 24 and lives in Texas. I'll tell you more in the morning. She is going to share photos and other information by email."

My sleep was sporadic to say the least. *Is this for real? What is the family like and what will they be asking us? If only we would have known something before she died so we could've seen her.*

The initial information Kristina shared with Patricia during the three-hour telephone conversation was about her family as she knew it. Piecing the information together revealed Mom had met a truck driver named Don Moore, and had a daughter out of wedlock named Linda Sue. Linda was born October 31, 1953, seventeen months after Mom left us. Mom found out Don had another family in Texas so did not want anything to do with him.

After my dad died I found a sheet out of a tablet with Dad's handwriting stating Mom met a man named Don Moore, a truck driver for Indianhead Trucking. Perhaps that is why Dad hit her that night in 1952, or maybe that is why Mom expressed fear in the letter I received from her.

In conversations, Kim, Linda's daughter, said our mom told her she had no idea Don was married when she met him and only found out after she became pregnant. They later learned he actually didn't marry until 1967. Mom first went to Illinois and then to Ohio, but we don't know for how long. It was in Ohio where she obtained a new social security number, saying hers had been destroyed in a fire. At that time, she changed her last name to Sterling. I didn't think it was possible to obtain two different social security numbers, in a lifetime but I guess you can.

At some point, Don contacted Mom and arranged for her and Linda to move to Houston, Texas, date unknown, so he could see them more. According to Kim, he never supported Mom and Linda. She raised Linda alone and when Linda married, she moved in with them. Linda and Larry had a daughter Kimberly, born August 18, 1970. Kimberly had two daughters, Kristina, born May 30, 1987, and Alecia Nicole, born March 24, 1997. We would not have the chance to meet our half-sister; Linda died of a lung condition in 2004.

Kim said our mom and Don had a broken relationship over the years until his death in 1997. Kim said she knew from the age of eleven that Don was not good for her grandma. She said she called him Grampa but he was Don in her mind. She shared she had a hard time liking him from an early age; he was bossy and an unpleasant presence, but on the good side, she had a "beautiful mother and grandma."

Mom never told Linda, Kim, or Kristina about her life from 1936 to 1952. She shared her childhood memories and divulged her maiden name of Debovik. As Patricia said," Thank God for Ancestry.com and Kristina's knowledge of Mom's maiden name or this all would not have been possible."

*   *   *

Patricia's persistence in wanting to know about Mom was a factor. Patricia was the youngest child and had the least amount of memories, which contributed to her quest for answers. I recall when she was sixteen and came from La Crosse to Madison to spend a weekend with Mike and me. One night during that weekend, after I had settled down, I felt a nudge on my shoulder. I opened my eyes, thinking one of the kids needed something, but it was Patricia, "Rosie, tell me everything you know about our mom." Mike was on his shift at the fire station so I said to her, "Climb in. I'll do the best I can."

I talked; she listened. I can only assume what I might have told her, but it would have gone something like this: *She liked calling you Patricia, and at night before you went to sleep she would give butterfly kisses. Our mom loved nature and animals. Holidays were special to her—for Valentine's Day she would help us make homemade cards using lacy, paper doilies and heart cut-outs, and during the Easter season she always made hot-cross buns on Holy Saturday, and a cake in the shape of a lamb on Easter. May Day we would make May baskets and hang them on the door of a favorite neighbor. She was an excellent cook, and loved entering drawing contests.* (The love of cooking and drawing is so ironic because Patricia is a gourmet cook and a well-known artist in her community. Mom would have been so proud of her.)

Mom often wished she was a boy in her years growing up because boys could do things girls were not allowed to do, like baseball and ski-jumping.

In fifteen years I never heard Mom raise her voice. She was a gentle spirit.

I hope I told Patricia how our mom loved her babies. Being the oldest I have the memory of her being pregnant and saying, "Rose, come over here, feel my tummy," as she guided my hand across her bulging abdomen. "That is your baby sister or baby brother's little foot." It was magical.

Patricia, being an inquisitive teenager, most likely asked me some questions that brought memories to the surface, resulting in tears.

*   *   *

I felt like I was walking in dense fog following the news about Mom, knowing it would eventually become clear. There were phone calls back and forth between my brother and sisters, all of us bewildered. My emotions were that of sadness and happiness and everything in between.

I wanted answers but was hesitant at first to call Kristina to ask questions. I did send her an email the next day:

Kris, I have been praying for 59 years that one day I would find out about my mother. I thank you so much for looking on the internet and then calling Patricia. I am Rose Eleanor, the oldest of your great-grandmother's children. I will have a Mass of Thanksgiving said at my church, and will be contacting you soon to talk, but today I just have to savor the news. It fills me with many emotions and of course questions. Thank you again so much and may God bless you.

Kristina's birthday was on May 30 and I signed the card, Great-Aunt Rose, and asked if it was OK. I received an email with a *thank you* and a *yes*.

On June 12, Patricia and I received photos by email from Kristina of our mom and her other family. The family resemblance was striking. The photos canceled out any doubts about the reality of the situation. I sent photos of the Debovik farm, and of Mom's sister, Isabel. Three days later Kristina sent more photos, one that brought me to tears. It was a photo the family found in Mom's belongings after she died, which they could not identify. It was my eighth-grade photo, creased and worn.

Chapter 25
Closure

As I gazed out the airplane window, I saw the Dallas airport spread out below. There was a story down there waiting to emerge. *Would we leave Texas with the closure we were looking for?* Mary and Susan were sitting beside me. I wondered what they were thinking, and I thought about Rita flying from Toronto, Ontario, alone with her thoughts. I wished it would have worked out for my brother, Fred, and my sister, Barbara, to be part of this trip. It had been five months since we learned about Mom, and I had a need to find out all I could about Mom's life since 1952. The plan was for us to be met at the airport by Kim and Kristina, and our sister, Patricia, who had traveled from Alaska with Bob, by motorhome a few days earlier.

As the plane touched down I looked over at Mary and Susan, "We're here." I reached over and squeezed their hands. If anticipation could have triggered the oxygen masks, mine would have dangled above me.

We entered the airport terminal and headed for the bagage claim. We had exchanged photos and emails but thought to myself, *This was the real deal.* And then I saw Patricia, Kim, and Kristina. The family resemblance was…there was no doubt, we were related. "Patricia, we made it." We hugged and I turned to Kristina ready to hug her, then backed up a minute, my hands already on her shoulders, "We are a hugging family."

"We are, too," she answered with the most beautiful smile on her face, "and welcome to Texas."

I turned to Kim, who seemed a bit more reserved than her daughter, but her arms were extended and ready for a hug.

"I'm Rose, the oldest."

Mary and Susan introduced themselves and I think we all acknowledged that without Kristina's inquisitiveness, we wouldn't have had this moment. We thanked her.

As we gathered up our luggage Patricia told us the motor home was parked and we could sit and wait until Rita's flight arrived. While waiting for Rita we looked over maps of the Lewisville area (a suburb of Dallas), made plans for our three days, and just chatted. Our conversations were relaxed.

We all stood at the foot of the escalator and greeted Rita as she appeared. The look on her face was happy anticipation. I noticed an airport employee standing to the side with a smile and a look on his face that said, "I'm not sure what is going on but I think it is special." More hugs, introductions, and expressions of sadness because of Fred and Barbara not being there. Barbara and her husband, Woody, visited the next spring while in Texas visiting their three sons who live in the Austin area. Fred hopes to meet them in the future.

After leaving the airport all of us went to a place called The Saltgrass Steakhouse for supper. Kristina would share with me a few years later that she was unable to quit staring at me because *my resemblance to Mema was so intense to her.*

We were tired after our travel day but invigorated after meeting Kim and Kristina. We discussed how emotional the next day would be visiting Mom's burial site. We were not only having closure over her 1952 disappearance, but also of her death in 1998. It was strange planning a memorial service thirteen years later.

Kristina came back in the morning to take me to the airport car rental and also gave directions to St. Phillip the Apostle Catholic Church and the cemetery where Mom was buried, as well as directions to her mother's home, where we would be going for supper.

As we pulled up to the church Patricia and Bob were standing outside their motorhome. We greeted one another and headed for the entrance. Bob stayed back recognizing the significance of the day for my sisters and me, a beautiful gesture on his part. Mass wasn't being said but there was a small chapel where one could sit in silent reflection. I sat for a short time but had to leave when my emotions swallowed me up. When I went outside, I sat down next to Bob who was sitting on a bench, and opened my soul, "Bob, I've waited so long for closure. I didn't expect it to be so difficult. I wanted to see her alive." I don't recall how Bob answered me but I do know I was comforted. Bob has the gift of great eye contact, and I likely saw his caring.

When my sisters came from the chapel their faces told me they had a special moment, a look that said, *I want to speak but I'm speechless.*

On the church grounds was a beautiful sculpture entitled Mary Our Mother by Juhlin, 1998. Her hair was windswept, her face compassionate, she was barefoot, and one of her hands was extended as though welcoming us. We were brought to tears by the beauty of the sculpture. If Mary the statue could have spoken, she would have said, "Go, say your goodbyes to your mother. She is at peace and you will be as well. God is with you."

A paved path lined with roses, irises, and decorative shrubs took us past Stations of the Cross and a waterfall feature, leading us to a labyrinth. I had walked a labyrinth in the past and was pleased to see it. The labyrinth circle has a network of paths one must follow, starting from the outside and ending in the center. Before you begin you think of one thought or problem you want to concentrate on. By the time you slowly walk the maze (about twenty minutes), you've come to some realization, or answer, or sense of peace. I reflected on my 56-year journey of waiting for closure, and thanked God for taking good care of us.

As we were leaving the church grounds we saw the priest. We gave him a brief summary of our lives and why we were in Texas. We shared that our mother had been raised Catholic, however she quit going to a Catholic church after a priest in Ohio denied her assistance when she was pregnant with Linda. Later in her life she was part of a different denomination. The priest said he was going to see about getting permission to do a Catholic blessing at her gravesite. This would happen at a later date. We thanked him and left for the cemetery.

An impressive tree, massive in size, made a statement in the middle of the cemetery. As we made our way to Mom's gravesite we stopped chatting, our footsteps and postures showing reverence. We were too emotional to speak, reaching to embrace each other, handing someone a tissue, or saying it was OK to cry, smile, or be silent. We were touched by the inscription on Mom's tombstone: *One Pearl of Great Price-Matthew 13:46.*

In planning our trip, Rita suggested we bring a vial of soil to sprinkle on the site. Fred and Barbara sent soil. Rita also brought seven red, flower-shaped candles. We lit the candles, placed a photo of Barbara, Fred and Shirley against the gravestone, and sprinkled in turn the soil. Patricia placed an African violet on top of the gravestone and planted two flowering plants on either side.

We recited in unison an ancient prayer Rita thought appropriate:

> TITLE: ALL IS WELL
> BY HENRY SCOTT HOLLAND (1847-1918)
> CANON OF ST. PAUL'S CATHEDRAL
> Death is nothing at all.
> I have only slipped into the next room.
> I am I and you are you.
> Whatever we were to each other, that we are still.
> Call me by my old familiar name.
> Speak to me in the easy way which you always used.
> Put no difference in your tone,
> Wear no forced air of solemnity or sorrow.
> Laugh as we always laughed at the little jokes we enjoyed together.
> Play, smile, think of me, pray for me.
> Let my name be ever the household word that it always was.
> Let it be spoken without effect, without the trace of shadow on it.
> Life means all that it ever meant.
> It is the same as it ever was, there is unbroken continuity.
> Why should I be out of mind because I am out of sight?
> I am waiting for you, for an interval, somewhere very near,
> Just around the corner.
> All is well.

We then sang a song Mom had taught me:

> M is for the million things she gave me
> O means only that she's growing old
> T is for the tears she shed to save me

H is for her heart of purest gold
E is for her eyes with love-light shining
R means right she'll always be
Put them altogether they spell Mother
A word that means the world to me.

At the end of the ceremony, we had our individual time to walk the cemetery grounds and grieve in our own way. *Mom, I'm standing under a most regal tree in the cemetery where you are buried. I feel comfort standing under its massive branches. It has been thirteen years since you died of lung cancer, and a long wait but I'm grateful to the Lord above for this day. We have met Kristina and Kim. Today we are invited to Kim and Sonny's for a visit and supper. I brought the letter you wrote to me so long ago. I am going to share it with Kim.*

Chapter 26
Filling in the Spaces of Mom's Life

"**I** don't know who is who, but," he said as he pointed to me, "your walk and mannerisms are just like Mema's." Mema was the endearing name they gave our mother.

We had just entered the home of Sonny and Kim Wagner and were warmly greeted by them and their daughters, Kristina and Alecia. Since we had met Kim and Kristina at the airport, we introduced ourselves one by one to Sonny and Alecia. Sonny looked very much a Texan in his western hat. There was a flurry of hugs, smiles, tears, and expressions of, "Can you believe this!" Alecia looked so much like Rita's daughter, Tamara; the resemblance cemented the fact we were family. Kristina, full of smiles, announced her fiancé, Justin, would be joining us later in the day.

The Wagner home felt comfortable and welcoming. Wonderful smells were coming from the kitchen. "Whatever you're cooking smells great."

Kim responded, "It was your mom's favorite."

I interrupted. "I'm sure it must be chicken and dumplings."

"Yes, it is, and for dessert, another of her favorites, peach cobbler."

Our mom loved to cook. Kim said Mom owned her own restaurant called the Dairy Mart in Crandall, Texas. After a year or so she was robbed several times and couldn't recover.

Years later she learned the robbery was done by a son of one of her employees.

Kim and Kristina were quick to offer us a beverage and snacks. We congregated in the kitchen area for a few minutes, talking about our visit to the cemetery and how special it was. I presented Kristina with a music box inscribed with the word FAMILY on it as a token gift for contacting us, and Patricia had given Kim a chain with a beautiful cross on it.

Kristina led us to the family room and pointed out Mom's bible on the shelf. "Most kids learn the ABC's when they are small; I did that, but Mema also taught me the books of the Bible." When we were sharing information prior to coming to Texas, Kim had told us when she was five she came home from the Christian school she attended reciting the books of the Bible. It was then our mom decided they all needed to start going to church. She let her son-in-law, Larry, choose the church, and Mom, with Kim's help, started learning the books of the Bible. At night as they were settling down for bedtime Kim would say Genesis, and our mom would say Exodus, etc. Larry became an ordained minister and performed the wedding of Kim and Sonny.

We women seated ourselves in the family room while Bob and Sonny chatted on the patio. Kim included herself in the conversation from the kitchen. I shared how Mary, Fred, and I, being the oldest when Mom left, had the visual memories of Mom, unlike Barbara, Rita, and Patricia, who were too little to remember. Kristina stood up and called out, "Mom, don't we have a Christmas tape from when Mema was alive? She should be on the one from 1997, the Christmas before she died."

"You can look but it probably won't be very lengthy."

"Just a glimpse would be worth it," said Patricia with a hopeful look on her face. Rita nodded in agreement.

"Give me a minute. I'll see if I can locate it."

Kristina found the tape, and you could have heard a pin drop as she inserted it into the video player. We intently watched, and Mom was visible for a second, but only a side view. Kristina said, "Just wait. There may be more." And she was there, looking right at the camera and then covering her face with her hand. Kristina chuckled, "She didn't like us filming her." Her hair was snow-white and so thick for her age of 82, her face peppered with age spots but still beautiful. And then she was gone.

Kristina reversed the film and I took a still photo with my camera. I knew I needed to excuse myself when I glanced around the room and saw the emotional looks on my sister's faces. Mom was with us for a moment. I felt sadness at not seeing Mom before she died, happiness knowing how much she was loved by Linda and Larry, Kim and Sonny, and Kristina and Alecia, and maybe a little jealousy at seeing her on their video and not ours. I darted out of the room, almost running to the front door, as tears rolled down my face. I walked around the block trying to absorb the feelings of the past 24 hours.

When I returned everyone was outside on the patio. The mood became lighter as we shared stories back and forth about Mom. She never lost her love for fishing, sometimes spending five or more hours at a time at her favorite fishing spot on Lewisville Lake in Lewisville, Texas. Crappies were her favorite panfish. She would say, "Fishing for supper," and sometimes that was the honest truth. Kim and Kristina said now that they knew Mom had seven other children, the lake was probably her quiet place where she could be alone with her thoughts. They also shared that at times Mom would be moody, and now wonder if on those days it was one of our birthdays. Kim was gifted in relating stories about Mom and we were like sponges absorbing everything she said. It was comforting to know the mom they knew and loved was the same mom I had for fifteen years.

Prior to our coming to Texas, Kim had also shared info by email: Mom loved black coffee and toast and butter; card games, especially canasta and pinochle; drawing which she called scratching, scrawling, or scribbling; crocheting; and houseplants. *I remember when Mom would use toothpicks to pierce the sides of a yam and suspend it over a glass of water with the bottom inch touching the water, and after several weeks have a beautiful plant emerge.*

Kim shared that our mom had several surgeries in her lifetime, the major one a hysterectomy after Linda was born, due to cervical cancer. She also had gallbladder, appendix, tonsil, and dental surgery. She would joke there wasn't anything else they could take from her. She suffered a broken hip, but the family said it did not stop her. She would scoot on the floor if necessary to get around. I remember I was the same way when I broke my leg.

We had a buffet line through the kitchen filling our plates with chicken and dumplings. The first bite transported me back to my childhood; the aroma, the taste was all there—the only difference was that it was made by Mom's granddaughter. We now have a copy of the recipe. The peach cobbler was the exclamation point!

Our Mother's Chicken & Dumpling Recipe

Chicken & Broth:
1 whole chicken
½ cup celery stalk and leaves
1 carrot, quartered
½ an onion

2 Tbs Lawrey's Season Salt
1 Tsp. pepper
1 Tsp garlic powder
1 bay leaf
1 Tsp salt

Dumplings:
3 cups flour
1 Tsp. salt
4 heaping Tbs. Crisco
1 cup chicken broth

Place whole chicken in pot and cover with water. Cook on medium high.
Add celery, carrot, and onion.
Cover and boil for 30 minutes.
Add season salt, pepper, garlic powder, bay leaf, and salt.
Boil for another 30 minutes.
During that time, you might need to add more water and/or seasonings to taste.
Remove chicken from broth and set aside to cool.
Strain broth. Set aside 1 cup of broth to cool.
Place the rest of the broth back on the stove to make the dumplings.

Dumplings:
Mix flour and salt in a medium mixing bowl. Add Crisco. Cut the Crisco into the flour using a pastry blender, making sure no white flour can be seen.
Add a cup of broth little by little until a ball of dough is formed.
Spread some flour out on the table and roll the dough out very thin.

Cut into strips about 1 x 2 inches and drop into the broth one piece at a time and in different places to keep them from sticking to each other.

While the dumplings are cooking, remove the skin and debone the chicken. Shred the chicken into bite-sized pieces and add to the dumplings.

Let stand to thicken.

Before returning to the hotel we took group photos that included all of us: Kim, Sonny, Kristina, Alecia, Trent, a son of Sonny's from a prior relationship, and his wife Melissa and little boy, Hayden, and the family dog, Rosco.

We made plans for the next day, followed by many hugs and expressions of gratitude. We said our goodbyes to Patricia and Bob who were continuing their motorhome trip early the next morning.

*   *   *

The following day the four of us in one car, and Kim, Kristina, and Alecia in another, drove to the church and walked the labyrinth together. We went to the cemetery to retrieve the flower-shaped candles as a souvenir and to stop for a moment, as new family members, at Mom's grave. And then it was as though Mom was speaking to us—a large flock of white snow geese flew overhead, the deep blue Texas skies a perfect backdrop, and hearing not only the sound of honking but the sound of wings flapping. That moment was meant to be.

We drove to Lewisville Lake. As I entered the parking lot, I felt without a doubt that this was where Mom came not only to fish but to be alone with her thoughts. The lake stretched out far out into the distance; it is one of the largest lakes in north Texas with 233 miles of shoreline. Mallards and coots were swimming along the shoreline, some were resting on the piers. Many wooden benches lined the piers, some piers open and others with a roof. I pictured Mom sitting on one of them when she fished, or maybe she preferred the grassy embankment. I handed my camera to Kim or Kristina and had them take a couple of Mary, Susan, Rita, and myself sitting on one of those benches.

We went back to the hotel to pack for our departure the next day, but agreed to meet later in the day to go to supper together at Joe's Crab Shack. The crab was delivered to the table in a large metal bucket. My sister, Mary, had never eaten crab legs before so was instructed by Kristina how to go about it. Mary's comment was, "It seems like a lot of mess and work." There is some truth to that but so worth it. We followed up the meal with a Texas-sized ice-cream drink.

We returned to the house, took more photos, had a group hug, shed tears of joy, expressed our gratitude, and felt closure. I would leave Texas with a peaceful heart.

I did share the letter from Mom with Kim. I sat next to her while she read. She stopped reading, dropped the letter to her lap, and seemed deep in thought. "Now it all makes sense."

"And what is that?" I asked.

"Those last days when Mema was in hospice, she mumbled words we didn't understand."

With tears in her eyes Kim said, "Now I know she was saying, 'Buy the little ones a dolly.' "

Epilogue

Writing my memoir has been a journey, an enlightening journey.

My character, myself, is three persons: the fifteen-year-old girl devastated by the disappearance of her mom, who had to assume many responsibilities; the adult who made it her mission to remain a family even when separated; and the person I am today, who gained new perspectives about Mom and Dad. In today's world with the availability of marriage support groups, counseling, and agency assistance, my story as written may not have happened, but it did.

I feel blessed that I was non-judgmental and for the most part had a positive attitude. Was I hurt because my mom left? Of course, I was, but I couldn't judge her when I didn't understand the reasons. I know in the beginning I thought it was Dad's fault, based on the fear Mom expressed in her letter, but I didn't know the whole story then and I don't know it now.

My prayer for my mom was that she had someone to love and for someone to love her. She had that love from us, and from Linda and Larry, Kimberly and Sonny, and Kristina and Alecia.

There was power and revelation in reading the letters Dad had saved, letters I had written to him over a span of 25 years. I wish I could thank him. The content of the letters confirmed the dedication and commitment I had to my brother and sisters, as well as Dad's commitment to us.

He cared. He was a wonderful grampa to his grandchildren. He saved all the letters and cards he received from them and none of their letters to him ever went unanswered.

Did my dad ever have someone to tell how he felt, or was his bottle of beer his only confidant?

Did he understand why Mom left? Did he love her or hate her?

I wish he'd had closure as we did. It was apparent he never stopped wondering about her. I remember an occasion in 1976 when he was visiting us and asked, "Rosie, do you know where your mom is?"

"Sorry, Dad, I don't."

I was happy he asked because I knew it still concerned him. I was sad to think he thought I might have known but didn't tell him. But had I known, I really don't know what my answer would have been.

Today, I like who I am, but in writing this memoir and thinking about my life, I know my mom's disappearance did have an effect on me. It's hard to explain, but I often found myself or maybe I *placed* myself on the outside looking in, always looking for her. It became a habit after 59 years.

I am grateful to the foster parents: Warren and Christy Bruns (my foster parents for three months while I worked for them), Larry and Margaret Mary Alland, Joe and Coletta Stevens, Frank and Dorothy Zahn, Jack and Margaret Marcou, and Don and Esther Senn. Back in the fifties foster home placement was long-term so it was like being adopted. They became my siblings' parents and my extended family. As of this writing they have all passed away except for Margaret Marcou.

When my brother and sisters are together, the conversation often centers on the deep bond we have. It is a bond of love, family, deep tenderness for one another, respect, appreciation for each other's strengths, and acceptance of our differences. It feels right—it is good. We ask ourselves if we would be so blessed if we had grown up "normally"—whatever that is. We miss our sister, Barbara, who was killed in a motor vehicle accident on July 24, 2014, on her way to volunteer at a food pantry. We are comforted by remembering the beautiful things said about her by so many people at her funeral in Minocqua, Wisconsin. Barbara was dedicated to her family, church, and community.

Lynn Davidman, a professor of sociology, found in a three-year study of thirty men and women who had lost their mothers, many go on to careers such as nursing. I mention this because four of us became nurses, and the three who are not are very caring individuals.

In previous chapters, I have mentioned our seventeen grandchildren. We have twelve great-grandchildren: Taliyah, Kailee, Payten, Cali, Ayla, Brooklynn, Calen, Cashton, Emery, Bently, Kinsley, and Kinzley; my love to these children and children of the future. Our family is saddened by the unexpected death of our grandson, Tyler Bingham, on June 10, 2017.

With a family this size, there have been challenges such as broken marriages and drugs and alcohol, but there has been much to celebrate as well. I learned early in life the importance of a good attitude and strong faith. Some of the family call me "the Rock," and I accept that compliment.

In that letter of December 1952, Mom said God would take care of us, and He did.

Acknowledgments

First and foremost, I thank God for all the angels he sent my way on my journey of life. I'm grateful to my parents who brought me into this world, and for my siblings Mary, Fred, Susan, Barbara, Rita, and Patricia. Thanks for sharing your memories, giving input, and critiquing some chapters. Barbara, I know you are not here in body to savor the completion of my memoir but I know you are here in spirit. [In 2014, Barbara died after her car was rear-ended and pushed into the path of a bus.]

One of the best things I did for myself was taking courses in Creative Writing and Women in Literature at UW Baraboo in 1996. Dave Cole was an exceptional instructor who showed genuine interest in what his students wrote. Dave, thanks for the written critiques; they were worth more than jewels.

Jackie Zenk, you gave me many gifts when you told me about the annual UW-Madison Writers' Institute: the welcoming face of Laura Kahl at the registration table, the wisdom and leadership of Laurie Scheer and Christine DeSmet, the knowledge shared by the presenters, and the opportunity to network with novice and seasoned writers.

Nathan Bransford, who was a keynote speaker at one of the conferences said, *"To get rid of self-doubt is unshakable love for your work."* Thank you, Nathan. Your quote motivated me many times to keep going.

I can't say enough about the writer's group I belong to, called JUST WRITE. Our bimonthly get-togethers helped me reach my goal of publishing my memoir. It was not only the critiques of written material but the emotional support, love, and encouragement, as well as being a part of the stories they are writing. Thank you, Jackie Zenk, for teaching me much about setting the scene by not forgetting the use of three or more of our five senses; Carol Showalter, retired teacher, for keeping me on my toes regarding punctuation, and Don Skarda, for giving me honest critiques and a man's perspective.

Kilbourn Library Book Club members, and librarians, Cathy Borck and Laura Gavinski, thank you for critiquing a couple of my chapters, and for your support.

Doris Marten and Jan Hess, I appreciate you reading my manuscript and giving me feedback.

A very special thank you to my sister, Patricia, and cousins, Art Lamberti and Marguerite Czajka, for information put on the *Family Tree Maker and Ancestry* sites, and to my half-niece, Kimberly Wagner, and half-great niece, Kristina (Wagner) Gressett, for being inquisitive about their grandmother / great-grandmother, who happened to be the mother of my siblings and I, but most of all for contacting us, or this memoir may not have been written.

When I began to write my story in 2012, my intent was to write it for my family. Thank you to my family, friends, and all the writers who encouraged me to share my story with others. You know who you are. To you I extend my gratitude.

And last but not least, a very special thank you to my hubby, Mike, for his unwavering support.

About the Author

Rose Bingham is a retired registered nurse. She graduated from the St. Francis school of Nursing in La Crosse, Wisconsin in 1958, and received her BSN from the University of Wisconsin in Madison in 1996. She has won numerous awards for her poetry and other writing. Her hobbies include photography, gardening, and travel. She is the proud mother of six, grandmother of seventeen, and great-grandmother of twelve. Rose resides in Wisconsin Dells with her husband, Mike, and her dog, Rylee.

Thanksgiving 2013 (from L to R) Rose, Mary, Fred, Susan, Barbara, Rita, and Patricia at the Bingham's home.

Portrait of my mother, painted by Patricia.

My father. Fred H. Steinmetz Photo taken June 1st, 1952 a Target Bluff, Camp Douglas, WI, by my mother, Eleanor Steinmetz.

(From L to R): Rita, Mom, Patricia, Susan, Barbara (1951).

(From L to R): Rose, Patricia, Front: Barbara, Susan, Rita (1951).

Dad, Mom and Fred in our front yard, Camp Douglas, WI (1952).

(From L to R): Mary, Fred, Susan, Barbara, my friend Barbara Brown, Rita (1952).

LeRoy

Aunt Mabel

Richard York

St. James Catholic Church and Rectory, Camp Douglas, WI

St. Michael's Orphanage, La Crosse, WI

Christmas at the orphanage. (L to R): Susan, Fred, Mary, Rose. (front) Barbara, Rita, Patricia (1954).

(L to R): Fred, Susan, Barbara, Rita, Patricia (summer of 1954).

Fred and Pepper

My high school
graduation photo
(1955).

To Reign at Camp Douglas Prom

ROSE STEINMETZ

DARWIN McCUMBER

Reigning over the Camp Douglas Junior Prom Friday evening, April 24, will be King Darwin McCumber and his Queen, Rose Steinmetz. The prom will be held at the Camp Douglas Community hall.

The Rose Ray Trio will furnish music for dancing from 9:00 to 1:00. The theme is "Stairway to the Stars."

Last year's prom royalty, JoDeen Wilkinson and George Termoen, will crown the King and Queen at 10:15 followed by the Grand March. Those in the Court of Honor are: Nancy Wedell and Jim Philps, Joyce Hess and Jerry Tormoen, Edith Kruschke and Harlan Madison, Joanne Billings and John Frohmader.

Shirley Hearth, the friend
I skipped school with.

My friend Barbara Brown.

My friend Barbara's Aunt
Irene and Uncle Ralph.

Relaxing on the
Milwaukee Clipper.

My friend Jeanette.

Christy Bruns and Millie.

Warren Bruns

Wayne Lawrence.

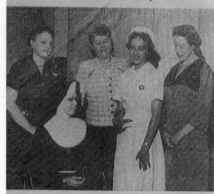

First To Win Loretta Morley Scholarship

Rose Steinmetz, pre-clinical student at St. Francis School of Nursing, is first winner of the Loretta Morley Nursing Scholarship conferred by the Zonta Club of La Crosse. An alumna of St. Michael's Home for Children, she was presented with the $500 scholarship Thursday, Sept. 1, a day after registering at the school. It covers her entire three-year course. Esther Domke, left, is Zonta service chairman, Mrs. Della Klenahs is president and the scholarship is named for Mrs. Loretta Morley, right, who founded it. Sister M. Francita is director of nursing at the school. To complete the raising of funds for the scholarship,

Zonta is giving an "Evening of Weddings" Monday, Oct. 10 at the Municipal Auditorium. Models in the show will be divided into five complete wedding parties. The scholarship is not the only project for which funds from the show will be used. Last year Zonta purchased a TV for La Crosse County Infirmary and previously furnished the entire recreation room at the Infirmary. This spring the club presented an electric water heater to the Girl Scout camp. Among other larger gifts was that of a projector to the YMCA.

—Tribune Photo

Receiving my nursing school scholarship.

Seve your daughter
Rose
1958

My nursing school
graduation (1958).

My 8th grade photo,
found in my mom's
belongings when she died.

Mike Bingham in Korea.

Dad saved the letters I had
written him.

Six sisters around the May Pole in Toronto, Ontario (2004).
(L to R): Rita, Barbara, Susan, Mary, Rose, and Patricia.

Mary, Patricia and Susan walking the labyrinth.

My half-sister Linda and Mom.
Linda (10/31/1953—8/22/2005)
Mom (11/14/1915—6/17/1998)

Mom's tombstone.

A glimpse of our mom on video.

Half-great-nieces, Alecia and Kristina; niece Kim.

(L to R): Mary, Kim, Rita, Alecia, Kristina, Susan, Patricia, Rose, and Rosco the Lab.

Photo of Mom in her later years, given to me by the Wagner family.

Grandma Debovik, Mauston, WI (1935).

Me (Rose) and Mom, 1st day of school (1943).

Photo of my mom as I last remember her.

Family photo (L to R, standing): Rose, David, Michael, Mark, Mike
(L to R, seated): Julie, Michelle, Mary (2008).

Celebrating Mike's and my 50thAnniversary with a mass said by Monsignor Felix Oehrlein at St. Cecelia Parish, Wisconsin Dells, December 20, 2008.

With our "other family" in Texas
(L to R, standing): Rose, Susan, Kim, Sonny, Kristina, Rita, Mary
(L to R, front): Trent, Melissa holding Hayden, Alecia (2011).

(L to R): Rita, Susan, Rose, Mary, Lewisville Lake, TX (2011).

(L to R): Mary, Rose, Susan, Rita, Lewisville Lake, TX (2011).

(L to R): Rita, Rose, Patricia, Susan, and Mary ,Standing by the "Mary" statue (2011).